2nd Edition

Web 3.0 Compatible

WEB TECHNOLOGIES

SERVLET, JSP, .NET, ASP.NET, PERL, XML, AJAX

Ajit & Praveen

Advanced Web Tehnologies

ACKNOWLEDGEMENT

This piece of study of Advanced Web Technologies is an outcome of the encouragement, guidance, help and assistance provided to me by my colleagues, Sr. faculties, Tech-friends and my family members.

Here, we are taking this opportunity to express our deep sense of gratitude to everybody whose roles were crucial in the successful completion this book, especially to our sr. students. This book benefited from discussions with many IT professionals over the three years it took me to write it.

Our primary goal is to provide a sufficient introduction and details of the Advanced Web (Web 3.0) Technologies including Servlet, JSP, PERL, ASP .NET , XML & AJAX so that the students can have an efficient knowledge about Advanced Web Technologies.. While reading this textbook, students may find the going somewhat tough in spite of our treating the topics in depth but in simple manner. In that case, reread the topic, if still it doesn't do the trick, then only you may need the help of expert. Any remaining errors and inaccuracies are our responsibility and any suggestions in this regard are warmly welcomed !

We would also like to thank those who provided the odd suggestion via email to us. All feedback was listened to and you will no doubt see some content influenced by your suggestions.

Finally, We would like to thank the Kindle Direct Publishing team and Amazon team for its enthusiastic online support and guidance in bringing out this book.

We hope that the reader likes this book and finds it useful in learning the concepts of Advanced Web Technologies.

Thank You !!

PREFACE

Share the knowledge!!

Strong the surroundings........

The study/learning of Advanced Web Technologies is an essential part of any computer science education and of course for the B.Tech / MCA / M.Tech courses of several Universities across the world. This textbook is intended as a text for an explanatory course of Advanced Web Technologies for Graduate and Post Graduate students of several universities across the world.

This text is an introduction to the complex world of the Advanced Web Technologies. This new edition has been thoroughly reviewed and revamped to reflect the new web design environment (Web 3.0). This book encapsulates rich practical hands-on experience in developing web applications, combined with teaching the subject for graduate/post-graduate students. The book is therefore a culmination of putting together what has been both practiced as well as preached, which is the one of the most compelling differentiators for this book. But what is more fascinating is the nature of the web itself. It can also be used for independent study by anyone interested in getting a broad introduction to a useful subset of the many technologies commonly used to develop commercial and recreational websites. This book covers knowledge of all web development programming languages like SERVLET, JSP, PERL, XML, XSL, .NET, ASP.NET, AJAX.

This book will help web application developers and software architects pick the right strategy for developing cross-platform applications that run on a variety of desktop computers as well as mobile devices. Through this book, we hope that you will see the absolute necessity of understanding which WEB TECHNOLOGY to use for a certain scenario. In all projects, especially those that are concerned with performance (here we apply an even greater emphasis on real-time systems) the selection of the wrong web technology can be the cause of a great deal of performance pain.

Within, you will find information on a variety of topics involved in the overall process of planning, designing, and finally creating a website; this background will help you understand how these pieces fit together, so you are better able to understand and contribute to a project and work with others on your team. My final note: never take the words of others as gospel; verify all that can be feasibly verified and make up your own mind. We hope you enjoy reading this book as much as we have enjoyed writing it.

Advanced Web Technologies
2nd Edition

For information about this title or to order other books and/or electronic media, contact the publisher:

Ajit Singh & Praveen Kumar

CONTENTS

	If, while, etc. File Input Print output Strings and Regular Expressions Subroutines Running External Programs References Terse Perl	
7	ASP .NET ASP.NET Coding Modules ASP.NET Page directives: Page Event and Page Life Cycle PostBack and CrossPage Posting ASP.NET Application Compilation Models ASP.NET Server Controls HTML Controls Validation Controls Building Databases	131
8	XML Syntax DTDs and XML Schema XPath XSLT Sax and DOM	166
9	AJAX Introduction Technologies Functioning Example Application AJAX Database Application	180

## 1

INTRODUCTION

INTRODUCTION

Web technologies are the various tools and techniques that are utilised in the process of communication between different types of devices over the internet.Web Technology is essential today because Internet has become the number one source to information, and many of the traditional software applications have become Web Applications. Web Applications have become more powerfull and can fully replace desktop application in most situations.

Thats why you need to know basic Web Programming, including HTML, CSS and JavaScript. To create more powerful Web Sites and Web Applications you also need to know about Web Servers, Database Systems and Web Frameworks like PHP, ASP.NET, etc.

THE WORLD WIDE WEB

World Wide Web

The Web's historic logo designed by
Robert Cailliau

The **World Wide Web**, abbreviated as **WWW** and commonly known as **the Web**, is a system of interlinked hypertext documents accessed via the Internet. With a web browser, one can view web pages that may contain text, images, videos, and other multimedia and navigate between them by using hyperlinks. Using concepts from earlier hypertext systems, British engineer and computer scientist Sir Tim Berners-Lee, now the Director of the World Wide Web Consortium, wrote a proposal in March 1989 for what would eventually become the World Wide Web. He was later joined by Belgian computer scientist Robert Cailliau while both were working at CERN in Geneva, Switzerland.

"The World-Wide Web (W3) was developed to be a pool of human knowledge, which would allow collaborators in remote sites to share their ideas and all aspects of a common project."

History of the World Wide Web

Arthur C. Clarke was quoted in Popular Science in May 1970, in which he predicted that satellites would one day "bring the accumulated knowledge of the world to our fingertips" using an office console that would combine the functionality of the xerox, telephone, TV and a small computer so as to allow both data transfer and video conferencing around the globe.

In March 1989, Tim Berners- Lee wrote a proposal that referenced ENQUIRE, a database and software project he had built in 1980, and described a more elaborate information management system.

With help from Robert Cailliau, he published a more formal proposal (on November 12, 1990) to build a "Hypertext project" called "WorldWideWeb" (one word, also "W3") as a "web" of "hypertext documents" to be viewed by "browsers" using a client– server.

A NeXT Computer was used by Berners-Lee as the world's first web server and also to write the first web browser, WorldWideWeb, in 1990. By Christmas 1990, Berners-Lee had built all the tools necessary for a working Web: the first web browser (which was a web editor as well); the first web server; and the first web pages, which described the project itself.

WWW Prefix

Many web addresses begin with *www*, because of the long-standing practice of naming Internet hosts (servers) according to the services they provide. The hostname for a web server is often *www*, as it is *ftp* for an FTP server, and *news* or *nntp* for a USENET news server. These host names appear as Domain Name System (DNS) subdomain names, as in www.example.com. When a single word is typed into the address bar and the return key is pressed, some web browsers automatically try adding "www." to the beginning of it and possibly ".com", ".org" and ".net" at the end. For example, typing 'microsoft<enter>' may resolve to *http://www.microsoft.com/* and 'openoffice<enter>' to *http://www.openoffice.org*. This feature was beginning to be included in early versions of Mozilla Firefox.

The 'http://' or 'https://' part of web addresses *does* have meaning: These refer to Hypertext Transfer Protocol and to HTTP Secure and so define the communication protocol that will be used to request and receive the page, image or other resource. The HTTP network protocol is fundamental to the way the World Wide Web works, and the encryption involved in HTTPS adds an essential layer if confidential information such as passwords or bank details are to be exchanged over the public internet.

Standards

Many formal standards and other technical specifications and software define the operation of different aspects of the World Wide Web, the Internet, and computer information exchange.

Usually, when web standards are discussed, the following publications are seen as foundational:

Recommendations for markup languages, especially HTML and XHTML, from the W3C. These define the structure and interpretation of hypertext documents. Recommendations for stylesheets, especially CSS, from the W3C.Standards for ECMAScript (usually in the form of JavaScript), from Ecma International. Recommendations for the Document Object Model, from W3C.

Additional publications provide definitions of other essential technologies for the World Wide Web, including, but not limited to, Uniform Resource Identifier (URI), HyperText Transfer Protocol (HTTP)

Speed issues

Frustration over congestion issues in the Internet infrastructure and the high latency that results in slow browsing has led to an alternative, pejorative name for the World Wide Web: the World Wide Wait. Speeding up the Internet is an ongoing discussion over the use of peering and QoS technologies. Other solutions to reduce the World Wide Wait can be found at W3C.

Standard guidelines for ideal Web response times are:

- 0.1 second (one tenth of a second). Ideal response time. The user doesn't sense any interruption.
- 1 second. Highest acceptable response time. Download times above 1 second interrupt the user experience.
- 10 seconds. Unacceptable response time. The user experience is interrupted and the user is likely to leave the site or system.

Caching

If a user revisits a Web page after only a short interval, the page data may not need to be re-obtained from the source Web server. Almost all web browsers cache recently obtained data, usually on the local hard drive. HTTP requests sent by a browser will usually only ask for data that has changed since the last download. If the locally cached data are still current, it will be reused. Caching helps reduce the amount of Web traffic on the Internet. The decision about expiration is made independently for each downloaded file, whether image, stylesheet, JavaScript, HTML, or whatever other content the site may provide.

Thus even on sites with highly dynamic content, many of the basic resources only need to be refreshed occasionally. Web site designers find it worthwhile to collate resources such as CSS data and JavaScript into a few site-wide files so that they can be cached efficiently. This helps reduce page download times and lowers demands on the Web server.

Questions based on WWW:

Explain the invention of WWW?
What are the Advantage of WWW?
What were the speed issues caused by WWW?

WORLD WIDE WEB ARCHITECTURE

The *World Wide Web* (*WWW*, or simply *Web*) is an information space in which the items of interest, referred to as resources, are identified by global identifiers called Uniform Resource Identifiers (*URI*).

All TAG participants, past and present, have had a hand in many parts of the design of the Web. In the Architecture document, they emphasize what characteristics of the Web must be preserved when inventing new technology. They notice where the current systems don't work well, and as a result show weakness. This document is a pithy summary of the wisdom of the community.

This scenario illustrates the three architectural bases of the Web :

1. Identification: URIs are used to identify resources. In this travel scenario, the resource is a periodically updated report on the weather in Oaxaca, and the URI is "http://weather.example.com/oaxaca".

2. Interaction: Web agents communicate using standardized protocols that enable interaction through the exchange of messages which adhere to a defined syntax and semantics. By entering a URI into a retrieval dialog or selecting a hypertext link, Nadia tells her browser to perform a retrieval action for the resource identified by the URI. In this example, the browser sends an HTTP GET request (part of the HTTP protocol) to the server at "weather.example.com", via TCP/IP port 80, and the server sends back a message containing what it determines to be a representation of the resource as of the time that representation was generated. Note that this example is specific to hypertext browsing of information—other kinds of interaction are possible, both within browsers and through the use of other types of Web agent; our example is intended to illustrate one common interaction, not define the range of possible interactions or limit the ways in which agents might use the Web.

3. Formats: Most protocols used for representation retrieval and/or submission make use of a sequence of one or more messages, which taken together contain a payload of representation data and metadata, to transfer the representation between agents. The choice of interaction protocol places limits on the formats of representation data and metadata that can be transmitted. HTTP, for example, typically transmits a single octet stream plus metadata, and uses the "Content-Type" and "Content-Encoding" header fields to further identify the format of the representation. In this scenario, the representation transferred is in XHTML, as identified by the "Content-type" HTTP header field containing the registered Internet media type name, "application/xhtml+xml". That Internet media type name indicates that the representation data can be processed according to the XHTML specification.

The diagram shows the relationship between identifier, resource, and representation.

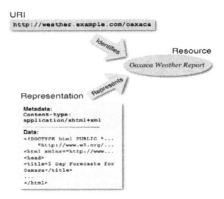

Global Identifiers
Global naming leads to global network effects.

Identify with URIs
To benefit from and increase the value of the World Wide Web, agents should provide URIs as identifiers for resources.

URIs Identify a Single Resource
Assign distinct URIs to distinct resources.

Avoiding URI aliases
A URI owner SHOULD NOT associate arbitrarily different URIs with the same resource.

Consistent URI usage
An agent that receives a URI SHOULD refer to the associated resource using the same URI, character-by-character.

Reuse URI schemes
A specification SHOULD reuse an existing URI scheme (rather than create a new one) when it provides the desired properties of identifiers and their relation to resources.

URI opacity
Agents making use of URIs SHOULD NOT attempt to infer properties of the referenced resource.

Reuse representation formats
New protocols created for the Web SHOULD transmit representations as octet streams typed by Internet media types.

Data-metadata inconsistency
Agents MUST NOT ignore message metadata without the consent of the user.

Metadata association
Server managers SHOULD allow representation creators to control the metadata associated with their representations.

Safe retrieval
Agents do not incur obligations by retrieving a representation.

Available representation
A URI owner SHOULD provide representations of the resource it identifies

Reference does not imply dereference
An application developer or specification author SHOULD NOT require networked retrieval of representations each time they are referenced.

Consistent representation
A URI owner SHOULD provide representations of the identified resource consistently and predictably.

Version information
A data format specification SHOULD provide for version information.

Namespace policy
An XML format specification SHOULD include information about change policies for XML namespaces.

Extensibility mechanisms
A specification SHOULD provide mechanisms that allow any party to create extensions.

Extensibility conformance
Extensibility MUST NOT interfere with conformance to the original specification.

Unknown extensions
A specification SHOULD specify agent behavior in the face of unrecognized extensions.

Separation of content, presentation, interaction
A specification SHOULD allow authors to separate content from both presentation and interaction concerns.

Link identification
A specification SHOULD provide ways to identify links to other resources, including to secondary resources (via fragment identifiers).

Web linking
A specification SHOULD allow Web-wide linking, not just internal document linking.

Generic URIs
A specification SHOULD allow content authors to use URIs without constraining them to a limited set of URI schemes.

Hypertext links
A data format SHOULD incorporate hypertext links if hypertext is the expected user interface paradigm.

Namespace adoption
A specification that establishes an XML vocabulary SHOULD place all element names and global attribute names in a namespace.

Namespace documents
The owner of an XML namespace name SHOULD make available material intended for people to read and material optimized for software agents in order to meet the needs of those who will use the namespace vocabulary.

QNames Indistinguishable from URIs
Do not allow both QNames and URIs in attribute values or element content where they are indistinguishable.

QName Mapping
A specification in which QNames serve as resource identifiers MUST provide a mapping to URIs.

XML and "text/*"
In general, a representation provider SHOULD NOT assign Internet media types beginning with "text/" to XML representations.

XML and character encodings
In general, a representation provider SHOULD NOT specify the character encoding for XML data in protocol headers since the data is self-describing.

Orthogonality
Orthogonal abstractions benefit from orthogonal specifications.

Error recovery
Agents that recover from error by making a choice without the user's consent are not acting on the user's behalf.

Web 2.0

Within a very short stint of 17 years since Tim Berners Lee came up with the concept of World Wide Web, the growth of Internet has become unimaginable. Initially the web pages on the Internet were static html pages and the hosting servers found it very easy to support innumerous web pages on a single server since the demand on the server due to the use of static web pages was very low.

But, of Late, websites have started using dynamic contents and the demand on the servers hosting those pages has increased enormously. Web 2.0 concept penetrates into the Internet right here.

Web 2.0 is providing the required support to host the collection of second-generation web applications/web pages that utilize the dynamic technologies like AJAX enabling the user to make dynamic updates in their web page and providing a bunch of value added services for the customer. Google continues to be the vanguard of this innovation of using web2.0 applications! Google Suggest, A9 search of Amazon, Gmail, Google Maps are a few web URLs that have initiated the growth of Web 2.0 technology over the past few years! Ad-on to this list are YouTube and MySpace. The list of websites that have adopted this technology as on date is much more.

In the year and a half since, the term "Web 2.0" has clearly taken hold, with more than 9.5 million citations in Google. But there's still a huge amount of disagreement about just what Web 2.0 means, with some people decrying it as a meaningless marketing buzzword, and others accepting it as the new conventional wisdom.

What is Web 3.0?

The Internet is a constantly evolving technology that continues to innovate. So far, we've experienced Web 1.0 and 2.0, and there's much discussion of what to expect from Web 3.0. Web 1.0 provided a static experience for users without the ability to create the content-rich sites we have today. Web 2.0 brought us together with social media and dynamic websites, but at the cost of centralization.

Web 3.0 (also known as Web3) is the next generation of Internet technology that heavily relies on machine learning, artificial intelligence (AI), and blockchain technology. The term was created by Gavin Wood, Polkadot's founder and the co-founder of Ethereum. While Web 2.0 focuses on user-created content hosted on centralized websites, Web 3.0 will give users more control of their online data.

Web 3.0 is the third iteration of the Internet that interconnects data in a decentralized way to deliver a faster and more personalized user experience. It is built using artificial intelligence, machine learning and the semantic web, and uses the blockchain security system to keep your information.

If you're anything like me, it's hard to imagine how the internet is going to top sites like Twitter and Facebook. But it's bound to happen and when you research Web 3.0, you find out it is going to be synonymous with the user's interaction with the web.

In Web 2.0 we focused on the users' interaction with others, now we are going to focus more on the users themselves, which is always a plus. But how is this going to happen?

Layers of Web 3.0

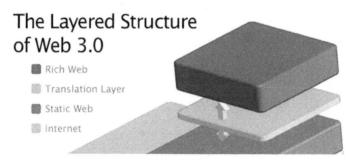

Web 3.0 is being referred to by experts as the semantic web; semantic meaning data driven. The data will come from the user and the web will essentially adjust to meet the needs of the user. For example, if you do a lot of searching for 'design blogs', you'll receive more advertisements related to design.

Also, when you search for other things, for example, 'computers', the web will keep in mind that you often search for design and may pull up search queries that combine 'design' and 'computers'.

Layers of Web 3.0

Whereas web 2.0 was primarily driven by the introduction of mobile, social and cloud technologies, web 3.0 is powered by three new layers of technological innovation:

- Edge computing

- Decentralization

- Artificial intelligence & machine learning

- Blockchain

1) Edge Computing

While currently commoditized personal computer technology was modified in data centers in web 2.0, the shift to web 3.0 is moving the data center out to the edge (i.e. edge computing) and sometimes straight into our hands.

Data centers are complemented by an array of advanced computing resources distributed among phones, laptops, appliances, sensors and cars, which will produce and consume 160 times more data in 2025 than in 2010.

2) Decentralized Data Network

Decentralized data networks enable various data generators to sell or trade their data without losing ownership, risking privacy or relying on intermediaries. As a result, decentralized data networks will have a long list of data providers in the growing 'data economy.'

For example, when you log in to an app using your email and password, or when you like a video or ask Alexa a question, all these activities are tracked and monitored by tech giants such as Google and Facebook to better target their advertisements.

However, in web 3.0, data is decentralized which means that users will own their data. Decentralized data networks enable various data generators to sell or trade their data without losing ownership, risking privacy or relying on intermediaries. It enables you to log in securely over the Internet without getting tracked by using Internet Identity.

3) Artificial Intelligence & Machine Learning

Artificial intelligence and machine learning algorithms have advanced to make valuable, and sometimes life-saving, predictions and acts.

When built on top of emerging decentralized data structures that provide access to a plethora of data that today's tech titans desire, the possible applications extend far beyond targeted advertising into areas such as:

- precision materials

- medication creation

- climate modeling

Although web 2.0 has similar capabilities, it is still primarily human-based, allowing for corrupt behaviors such as biased product evaluations, rigged ratings, human errors, etc.

For example, Internet review services such as Trustpilot allow customers to leave feedback on any product or service. Unfortunately, a firm may pay a large group of people to write excellent evaluations for its products or services.

4) Blockchain

In simple terms, blockchain is one more layer of technology behind web 3.0. More specifically, blockchain is the foundation of web3, as it redefines the data structures in the backend of the semantic web.

Blockchain is a decentralized state machine that deploys intelligent contracts. These smart contracts define the logic of an application for web 3.0. So anyone who wishes to build a blockchain application needs to deploy their application code on the shared state machine. (More on web 3.0 and blockchain below.)

Web 3.0 Architecture

There are primarily four elements (Proposed) in the architecture that make up web 3.0:

1. Ethereum Blockchain – These are globally accessible state machines maintained by a peer-to-peer network of nodes. Anyone in the world can access the state machine and write to it. Essentially, it is not owned by any single entity but, rather, collectively by everyone in the network. Users can write to the Ethereum Blockchain, but they can never update existing data.

2. Smart Contracts – These are programs run on the Ethereum Blockchain. These are written by the app developers in high-level languages, such as Solidity or Vyper, to define the logic behind the state changes.

3. Ethereum Virtual Machine (EVM) – The purpose of these machines is to execute the logic defined in the smart contracts. They process the state changes taking place on the state machine.

4. Front End – Like any other application, the front-end defines the UI logic. However, it also connects with smart contracts that define application logic.

Key Features of Web 3.0

The key features of web 3.0 are:

1. Open – It's 'open' in the sense that it's made with open-source software developed by an open and available community of developers and accomplished in full view of the public.

2. Trustless – The network offers freedom to users to interact publicly and privately without an intermediary exposing them to risks, hence "trustless" data.

3. Permissionless – Anyone, including users and providers, can engage without the need for permission from a controlling organization.

4. Ubiquitous – Web 3.0 will make the Internet available to all of us, at any time and from any location. At some point, Internet-connected devices will no longer be limited to computers and smartphones, as they are in web 2.0. Because of the IoT (Internet of Things), technology will enable the development of a multitude of new types of intelligent gadgets.

Benefits of Web 3.0?

Web2 is based on a server-client structure, meaning centralized private corporations control and own the data. The result is that these corporations have enormous monopoly power and create barriers to entry for potential competitors. All Web2 applications are controlled by centralized corporations, including the entire banking and financial system.

The Web3 has set out to break up the market power of these centralized players by replacing the centralized server-client infrastructure with distributed ledgers, the most common type being the blockchain. So instead of all data being stored on a centralized server, it will be scattered across a decentralized computer network. Centralized entities, which previously acted as intermediaries, will thus become obsolete.

Here is an example: Anyone sending money from one bank to another today uses the centralized servers of the respective banking providers. The banks act as intermediaries by carrying out the transaction. The user must hand over all the data to the banks involved and rely on them to execute the transaction correctly. The bank, of course, charges a fee for this service. This is Web2 banking.

In Web3 you can send your transaction via a decentralized blockchain such as the Bitcoin blockchain. This blockchain independently verifies the accuracy of the transaction through the use of mathematics and computing power. Unlike Web2, banks are no longer needed as intermediaries. That also means the user retains control over their data, and since there is no centralized actor making money from the transaction, there are no fees to pay.

In other words, Web3 should return data sovereignty and ownership rights to the user – that's at least the idea.

A huge benefit of Web 3.0 is the move towards being able to access data from anywhere. This is mainly being driven by the heavy usage of smart phones and cloud applications.

The idea here is to make sure that the user can access as much data as possible from anywhere, not just their home. Technology is trying to expand this idea in ways that allow TV's to pick up on user data, and allowing smart phones to access data on your computer.

For designers like myself who typically forget their jump drives, this is an amazing and useful advancement!

How does Web 3.0 work?

Web 3.0 aims to provide personalized and relevant information faster through the use of AI and advanced machine learning techniques. Smarter search algorithms and development in Big Data analytics will mean that machines can intuitively understand and recommend content. Web 3.0 will also focus on user-ownership of content and support for accessible digital economies.

Current websites typically display static information or user-driven content, like forums or social media. While this allows data to be published to the masses, it doesn't cater to specific users' needs. A website should tailor the information it provides to each user, similar to the dynamism of real-world human communication. With Web 2.0, once this information is online, users lose ownership and control.

Another key figure in the Web 3.0 concept is computer scientist Tim Berners -Lee, the World Wide Web inventor. He provided his idea of a web future in 1999:

> *"I have a dream for the Web [in which computers] become capable of analyzing all the data on the Web – the content, links, and transactions between people and computers. A "Semantic Web," which makes this possible, has yet to emerge, but when it does, the day-to-day mechanisms of trade, bureaucracy, and our daily lives will be handled by machines talking to machines.*

Berners-Lee's vision has since combined with Gavin Wood's message. Here, an ocean of decentralized information will be available to websites and applications. They will understand and use that data meaningfully with individual users. Blockchain acts as a solution for managing this online identity, data, and ownership in a fair manner.

The idea behind web 3.0 is to make searches on the Internet much faster, easier and more efficient to process even complex search sentences in no time.

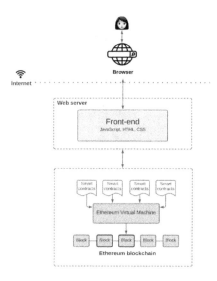

In a web 2.0 application, a user has to interact with its frontend, which communicates to its backend, which further communicates with its database. The entire code is hosted on centralized servers, which are sent to users through an Internet browser.

Web 3.0 has neither centralized databases that store the application state nor a centralized web server where the backend logic resides. Instead, there is a blockchain to build apps on a decentralized state machine and maintained by anonymous nodes on the web.

What makes Web 3.0 so unique?

Web 3's major benefit is that it seeks to solve the most serious issue that has arisen as a result of Web 2: the gathering of personal data by private networks, which is subsequently sold to marketers or potentially stolen by hackers.

Web 3's network is decentralized, meaning it is not controlled by a single organization, and the decentralized applications (apps) created on top of it are open.

Web 3.0's Effect on Design

So now that you have an idea of what Web 3.0 is and what it's going to be, we have to ask the most important question for us: what does that mean for design? Web 2.0 design was based around drawing attention and persuading your audience, because after all, web 2.0 made a huge deal about being able to purchase things online.

Web 2.0 wanted to generate excitement and get people to make a purchase and understand what they were doing. You want to make a purchase? Sure, then click this button. You want to join the mailing list? Great, then there's no question about clicking this button. That is the basis of Web 2.0 design.

Other elements were added to make things more fun and give a bit of style. The usage of linear gradients in web 2.0 is almost necessary.

Whatever color combination you desire, linear gradients are typically present from your background to your buttons. Other trends surfaced like various badges, rounded corners and a necessary usage of icons. But again the question remains, what can we expect for web 3.0. 3D Graphics is being used widely in websites and services in Web 3.0 such as online games, e-commerce, and portfolio website.

Put simply, the way the web looks will change hugely. We're already seeing a move towards 3D environments that even incorporate virtual reality. The metaverse is one area pioneering these experiences, and we're already familiar with socializing through 3D video games. The fields of UI and UX also work towards presenting information in more intuitive ways for web users.

Web 2.0 Design vs. Web 3.0 Design

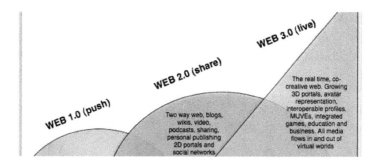

In web 2.0 we had to create design that was great for the web. I think in web 3.0, we will firstly have to create design that is going to be good not just for the web and the web browser, but for all sorts of media. With the growth in the usage of smart phones and tablets, people want more usage out of their items and to be able to access more things as best as possible.

Design will have to be able to translate in great quality across all sorts of technologies. Now while you can create two different websites (one for the web and one for mobile devices), designers and developers will have to kill two birds with one stone, by creating one website that will look good in both environments.

Also for Web 3.0, designers will continue to focus on making things simpler. The truth is, the designer has the absolute power to persuade viewers on where to look first and second and so forth and so on. By doing this the designer creates a hierarchy of importance, that should not be muddled by useless design.

Designers will continue to design so that content remains king by putting much focus on it and taking focus off non-content things such as logos and navigation bars.

Web 3.0 Design Trends?

Using these types of techniques plays into the increasing popularity of the minimalist design technique, where the focus is not necessarily making something as simple as possible, but making it as simplistic as possible.

Creating a site with non-flashy web elements makes the user HAVE to focus on the content of the site. Of course designers desire to design and will 'fancify' some things, but in Web 3.0, that isn't the main focus. The focus is to draw the viewers' eye to the content or other important information on the page.

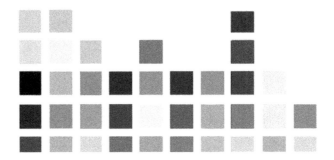

Many of the design trends used in Web 2.0 will only change by way of design, but not really the usage. The change in Web 2.0 to Web 3.0 is about how the internet is used, not really how it's seen (with the exception of mobile devices and such).

I believe designs will continue to get more and more minimalistic while maintaining a certain sense of beauty, but of course we will continue to use buttons and rounded corners and gradients. The design of Web 3.0 will be based on the way designers decide to design it and what becomes popular.

More on Web 3.0

Perhaps you desire to do your own research on the budding Web 3.0. Well we have provided some slide shows and videos that will get you started on the right path. Web 3.0 isn't here just yet, but when it does come, you should know what's coming at you!

The Web 3.0 Semantic Web

There is already a lot of work going into the idea of a semantic web, which is a web where all information is categorized and stored in such a way that a computer can understand it as well as a human.

Many view this as a combination of artificial intelligence and the semantic web. The semantic web will teach the computer what the data means, and this will evolve into artificial intelligence that can utilize that information.

Over time, machines have improved at understanding the data and content humans create. However, there is still a long way to create a seamless experience where semantics are fully understood. For example, the use of the word "bad" can, in some cases, mean 'good'. For a machine to understand this can be incredibly hard. However, with Big Data and more information to study, AI is beginning to understand better what we write on the web and present it intuitively.

The World Wide Virtual Web 3.0

This is a bit more of a far-fetched idea, but some have speculated that the popularity of virtual worlds and massively multiplayer online games (MMOG) like World of Warcraft might lead to a web based on a virtual world.

Kinset created a virtual shopping mall (see a video here) where users can walk into different stores and see the shelves populated with products. It isn't a stretch to see this expanded into an idea where users can interact with each other and walk into a wide variety of buildings, some of which might not even sell anything.

However, the idea that the entire web would evolve into one single virtual world with buildings, shops, and other areas to explore and people to interact with - while not unbelievable in a technological sense - has more than just technological hurdles to overcome. The virtual web would need to get the major websites on board and to agree to standards that would allow multiple companies to provide clients which, no doubt, would lead to some clients offering features that other clients don't, and, thus, fierce competition.

It would also increase the time it takes to bring a website into the virtual web since the programming and graphic design would be much more complex. This extra expense would probably be too much for smaller companies and websites.

This virtual web presents a few too many obstacles, but it should be kept in mind as a possible Web 4.0.

The Ever-Present Web 3.0

This isn't as much of a prediction of what the Web 3.0 future holds as it is the catalyst that will bring it about. The ever-present Web 3.0 has to do with the increasing popularity of mobile internet devices and the merger of entertainment systems and the web.

The merging of computers and mobile devices as a source for music, movies, and more puts the internet at the center of both our work and our play. Within a decade, internet access on our mobile devices (cell phones, smartphones, pocket PCs) has become as popular as text messaging. This will make the internet always present in our lives - at work, at home, on the road, out to dinner, the internet will be wherever we go.

Key features of Web 3.0

Web 3.0 is still far from complete adoption, but its core concepts are mostly already defined. The four topics below are commonly listed as the most important aspects of the Web 3.0 future.

Semantic markup

Over time, machines have improved at understanding the data and content humans create. However, there is still a long way to create a seamless experience where semantics are fully understood. For example, the use of the word "bad" can, in some cases, mean 'good'. For a machine to understand this can be incredibly hard. However, with Big Data and more information to study, AI is beginning to understand better what we write on the web and present it intuitively.

Blockchain and cryptocurrencies

Data ownership, online economies, and decentralization are essential aspects of Gavin-Wood's Web3 future. We'll cover the topic in more detail later on, but blockchain provides a tried and tested system to reach many of these goals. The power for anyone to tokenize assets, put information on-chain, and create a digital identity is a huge innovation that lends itself to Web 3.0.

3D visualization and interaction presentation

Put simply, the way the web looks will change hugely. We're already seeing a move towards 3D environments that even incorporate virtual reality. The metaverse is one area pioneering these experiences, and we're already familiar with socializing through 3D video games. The fields of UI and UX also work towards presenting information in more intuitive ways for web users.

Artificial intelligence

Artificial intelligence is the key to turning human-created content into machine-readable data. We're already familiar with customer service bots, but this is just the beginning. AI can both present data to us and sort it, making it a versatile tool for Web 3.0. Best of all, AI will learn and improve itself, reducing the work needed for human development in the future.

What makes Web 3.0 superior to its predecessors?

The combination of Web 3.0's key features will lead to a variety of benefits in theory. Don't forget that these will all depend on the success of the underlying technology:

1. No central point of control - Since intermediaries are removed from the equation, they will no longer control user data. This freedom reduces the risk of censorship by governments or corporations and cuts down the effectiveness of Denial-of-Service (DoS) attacks.

2. Increased information interconnectivity - As more products become connected to the Internet, larger data sets provide algorithms with more information to analyze. This can help them deliver more accurate information that accommodates the individual user's specific needs.

3. More efficient browsing - When using search engines, finding the best results have sometimes posed a challenge. However, they have become better at finding semantically-relevant results based on search context and metadata over the years. This results in a more convenient web browsing experience that can help anyone find the exact information they need with ease.

4. Improved advertising and marketing - No one likes being bombarded with online ads. However, if the ads are relevant to your needs, they could be useful instead of being an annoyance. Web 3.0 aims to improve advertising by leveraging smarter AI systems and targeting specific audiences based on

29

consumer data.

5. Better customer support - Customer service is critical for a smooth user experience for websites and web applications. Due to the massive costs, though, many web services that become successful struggle to scale their customer service operations. Using more intelligent chatbots that can talk to multiple customers simultaneously, users can enjoy a superior experience when dealing with support agents.

How does crypto fit into Web 3.0?

Blockchain and crypto have great potential when it comes to Web 3.0. Decentralized networks successfully create incentives for more responsible data ownership, governance, and content creation. Some of its most relevant aspects for Web 3.0 include:

1. Digital crypto wallets - Anyone can create a wallet that allows you to make transactions and acts as a digital identity. There's no need to store your details or create an account with a centralized service provider. You have total control over your wallet, and often the same wallet can be used across multiple blockchains.

2. Decentralization - The transparent spread of information and power across a vast collection of people is simple with blockchain. This is in contrast to Web 2.0, where large tech giants dominate huge areas of our online lives.

3. Digital economies - The ability to own data on a blockchain and use decentralized transactions creates new digital economies. These allow us to easily value and trade online goods, services, and content without the need for banking or personal details. This openness helps improve access to financial services and empowers users to begin earning.

4. Interoperability - On-chain DApps and data are increasingly becoming more compatible. Blockchains built using the Ethereum Virtual Machine can easily support each other's DApps, wallets, and tokens. This helps improve the ubiquity needed for a connected Web 3.0 experience.

Web 3.0 Use Cases

Siri & Alexa virtual assistants

Both Apple's Siri and Amazon's Alexa offer virtual assistants that check many of the Web 3.0 boxes. AI and natural language processing help both services better understand human voice commands. The more people use Siri and Alexa, the more their AI improves its recommendations and interactions. This makes it a perfect example of a semantically intelligent web app that belongs in the Web 3.0 world.

Connected smart homes

One key feature of Web 3.0 is ubiquity. This means that we can access our data and online services across multiple devices. Systems that control your home's heating, air conditioning, and other utilities can now do so in a smart and connected manner. Your smart home can tell when you leave, arrive, and how hot or cold you like your house. It can use this information, and more, to create a personalized experience. You can then access this service from your phone or other online devices, no matter where you are.

Advantages of Web 3.0

Web 3.0 will make the web more intelligent, secure and transparent, resulting in more efficient browsing and effective machine-human interaction. Here are the top advantages of the semantic web or web 3.0:

1) Data Privacy and Control

The end-users will get the most significant advantage of data encryption to protect their information from disclosure.

The encryption will be unbreakable in any given circumstance. It will prevent large organizations like Google and Apple from controlling or using people's personal information for their own interest.

Hence, users will gain complete ownership and privacy of their information.

2) Seamless Services

Decentralized data storage will ensure that the data is accessible to users in any circumstance. Users will get multiple backups, which benefits them even in the event of server failures.

Additionally, no entity or government organization will have the ability to stop any services or websites. Therefore, the possibility of account suspension and denial of distributed services will be reduced.

3) Transparency

Regardless of which blockchain platform end-users use, they will track their data and inspect the code behind the platform.

Nonprofits develop the majority of blockchain platforms, which means they provide an open-source blockchain platform that allows open design and development processes. This will help eliminate the dependency of users on the organization that develops the platform.

4) Open Accessibility to Data

The data will be accessible from anywhere and from any device. The idea is to increase data collection and its accessibility to users worldwide by allowing smartphones and other connected devices to access data on the computer if synced.

Web 3.0 will further expand the scale of interaction, ranging from seamless payments to richer information flows to trusted data transfers. This will happen because web3 will enable us to interact with any machine without passing through fee-charging middlemen.

5) Restrictionless Platform

Since the blockchain network is accessible to all, users can create their own addresses or interact with the network.

Users cannot be restricted on this network based on their gender, income, geographical location or sociological factors. This feature will make it easier for users to transfer their assets or wealth anywhere across the world in no time.

6) Single Profile Creation

With web 3.0, users do not need to create individual personal profiles for different platforms. A single profile will work on any platform, and the user will have complete ownership of any given information.

Without users' permission, no corporation can access their data or verify its accuracy. However, users have the choice to share their profiles and sell their data to advertisers or brands.

7) Enhanced Data Processing

Web 3.0 is beneficial for problem-solving and intensive knowledge creation tasks. It utilizes artificial intelligence to filter out valuable information from a huge quantity of data. Users will also benefit from its ability to conduct client demand forecasting and personalized customer service, necessary for flourishing businesses.

Disadvantages of Web 3.0

There are also several challenges associated with the implementation of web 3.0. Personal data management and reputation management issues will become more critical than ever.

Here are the top challenges associated with the implementation and usage of web3:

1) Requires Advanced Devices

Less advanced computers won't have the ability to provide the benefits of web 3.0. The devices' features and characteristics will need to be extended to make the technology reachable to more people globally. Considering the present scenario, only a limited number of people will be able to access web 3.0.

2) Web 1.0 Websites Will Become Obsolete

If web 3.0 becomes full-fledged on the Internet, any websites based on web 1.0 technology will become obsolete. The old technology is incapable of updating its features to match the new ones. This means those sites will be substantially more outdated and consequently lose a competitive edge over new sites.

3) Not Ready for Widespread Adoption

Web3 technology is more intelligent, efficient and accessible. Yet, the technology is not entirely ready for widespread adoption. Much work is needed on technology advancement, privacy laws, and data use to satisfy the user's needs.

4) Demand for Reputation Management Will Increase

With the easy availability of a user's information and less anonymity through web 3.0, reputation management will become a matter of concern more than ever. In other words, brands and companies will need to maintain their name, reputation and image online.

Companies will need to help customers acquire critical market intelligence, valuable business insights, compelling content and cutting edge internet marketing to stay ahead of competitors. Hence, reputation management will turn out to be more critical than ever.

5) Complicated Functionality

Web 3.0 is a difficult-to-understand technology for any new user, which makes them hesitant to use it. It is a combination of older-generation web tools with cutting-edge technologies, such as AI and blockchain, as well the interconnection between users and increasing Internet usage.

This will mean that only advanced devices will be able to handle web 3.0, making it difficult for any individual or business that cannot afford such devices. Because it is technically sound users who will gain the most from this technology, the complicated nature of web 3.0 is likely to slow down its popularity at a global level.

Why Web 3.0 Is Important for the Future

Web 3.0 is a system for users, designed by users in the form of creator-driven platforms. Here are the top reasons why web3 will become important in the coming years:

Less reliance on centralized repositories: Web 3.0 will attempt to make the Internet a diverse source so that hackers, leaks and reliance on centralized repositories are avoided. Using verifiable data scarcity and tokenized digital assets, there will be the possibility of users owning their own data and digital footprints. No platform will be held accountable for data usage.

More personalized interactions: Web 3.0 will become increasingly important in 2022, as most users continue to prioritize customized and individualized browsing encounters on the web.

Better search assistance powered by AI: There will be an increasing demand for humanized digital search assistants that are far more intelligent, pervasive and powered by semantics, blockchain and AI.

Reduced dependency on intermediaries: It will help disintermediate businesses, remove rent-seeking intermediaries, and give this value directly to the customers and providers in a network. Network users will work together to address previously hard-to-control problems by mutual ownership and governance of these new decentralized intelligence structures.

Rise in peer-to-peer connectivity: Through new Internet inventions, the connection between members and organizations will remain innately robust to keep in line with more adaptive peer-peer interaction and governance. With peer-to-peer connectivity, humans, businesses and machines will be able to share more data while maintaining greater privacy and security.

Enhanced trust: With the knowledge of the next Internet generation, we can reduce dependency on individual platforms to future-proof entrepreneurial and investment activity.

Web 3.0 and Metaverse

Metaverse is quite a buzzword since Facebook recently announced its new name 'Meta'. The idea is to showcase that the company is moving fast towards a Metaverse. However, Metaverse is still not a reality, but soon could be the next evolution of the Internet.

Metaverse generally refers to shared virtual world environments or a computer-generated environment, which is accessible to users via the Internet. It is a digital space that is designed as more lifelike by using "extended reality," the combination of augmented, virtual and mixed reality.

At the moment, people interact with each other through social media platforms or by using messaging applications. In the virtual space, users will have their own "character" that can walk around and interact with other users. They can communicate with one another through avatars, text messages, sounds, music videos, video games, etc.

Advanced Web Tehnologies

This means that people will have a 3D experience on the Internet. They can interact, play, work, or join in digital environments as if they are experiencing it in reality rather than just watching the content.

The role of web 3. 0 is vital in making Metaverse a reality, specifically if it uses blockchain technology. In other words, web3 will enable the virtual world to exist online and be accessible through a web browser.

Presently, Metaverse is more associated with virtual gaming, but this is not limited to only games. The scope of the web 3.0 Metaverse is much broader that also includes the education industry. For example, in an education Metaverse, users can enter an immersive classroom and interact with their teacher and other students.

In the future, web 3.0 and Metaverse will together proliferate in all aspects of society.

Questions based on WWW Architecture?
Explain the Architecture of WWW?
Explain the relationship of the three architectural bases of the Web?
Explain the next version of Web1.0?

WEB SEARCH ENGINE

A **web search engine** is designed to search for information on the World Wide Web. The search results are usually presented in a list of results and are commonly called *hits*. The information may consist of web pages, images, information and other types of files. Some search engines also mine data available in databases or open directories. Unlike Web directories, which are maintained by human editors, search engines operate algorithmically or are a mixture of algorithmic and human input.

How Search Engines Work

The term "search engine" is often used generically to describe both crawler-based search engines and human-powered directories. These two types of search engines gather their listings in radically different ways.

Crawler-Based Search Engines

Crawler-based search engines, such as Google, create their listings automatically. They "crawl" or "spider" the web, then people search through what they have found.

If you change your web pages, crawler-based search engines eventually find these changes, and that can affect how you are listed. Page titles, body copy and other elements all play a role.

Human-Powered Directories

A human-powered directory, such as the Open Directory, depends on humans for its listings. You submit a short description to the directory for your entire site, or editors write one for sites they review. A search looks for matches only in the descriptions submitted.

Changing your web pages has no effect on your listing. Things that are useful for improving a listing with a search engine have nothing to do with improving a listing in a directory. The only exception is that a good site, with good content, might be more likely to get reviewed for free than a poor site.

"Hybrid Search Engines" Or Mixed Results

In the web's early days, it used to be that a search engine either presented crawler-based results or human-powered listings. Today, it extremely common for both types of results to be presented. Usually, a hybrid search engine will favor one type of listings over another. For example, MSN Search is more likely to present human-powered listings from LookSmart. However, it does also present crawler-based results (as provided by Inktomi), especially for more obscure queries.

A List of All-Purpose Search Engines

1. Google

In the last few years, Google has attained the ranking of the #1 search engine on the Net, and consistently stayed there.

2. Yahoo

Yahoo is a search engine, subject directory, and web portal. Yahoo provides good search results powered by their own search engine database, along with many other Yahoo search options.

3. MSN Search

MSN Search is Microsoft's offering to the search world. Learn about MSN Search: its ease of use, cool search features, and simple advanced search accessibility.

4. AOL Search

Learn why so many people have chosen AOL Search to be their jumping off point when searching the Web. With its ease of use, simple accessibility, and nifty search features, AOL Search has carved itself a unique niche in the search world.

5. Ask

Ask.com is a very popular crawler-based search engine. Some of the reasons that it has stayed so popular with so many people are its ease of use, cool search features (including Smart Answers), and powerful search interface.

6. AlltheWeb

AlltheWeb is a search engine whose results are powered by Yahoo. AlltheWeb has some very advanced search features that make it a good search destination for those looking for pure search.

7. AltaVista

AltaVista has been around in various forms since 1995, and continues to be a viable presence on the Web.

8. Lycos

Lycos has been around for over ten years now (started in September of 1995), and has some interesting search features to offer. Learn more about Lycos Search, Lycos Top 50, Lycos Entertainment, and more.

9. Gigablast

Gigablast is a search engine with some interesting features, good advanced search power, and an excellent user experience.

10. Cuil

Cuil is a slick, minimalist search engine with a magazine look and feel. Cuil claims to have indexed over 121 billion Web pages, so it is quite a large search engine, plus, the search interface returns quite a few related categories and search terms that can potentially launch your search net quite a bit wider.

Questions based on Web Search Engine:
How Web Search Engines are useful for Web search?
How Web Search Engine works? List all the Search Engines?

Advanced Web Tehnologies

WEB CRAWLING

A web crawler is a relatively simple automated program, or script, that methodically scans or "crawls" through Internet pages to create an index of the data it's looking for. Alternative names for a web crawler include web spider, web robot, bot, crawler, and automatic indexer.

When a search engine's web crawler visits a web page, it "reads" the visible text, the hyperlinks, and the content of the various tags used in the site, such as keyword rich meta tags. Using the information gathered from the crawler, a search engine will then determine what the site is about and index the information. The website is then included in the search engine's database and its page ranking process.

Search engines, however, are not the only users of web crawlers. Linguists may use a web crawler to perform a textual analysis; that is, they may comb the Internet to determine what words are commonly used today. Market researchers may use a web crawler to determine and assess trends in a given market. There are numerous nefarious uses of web crawlers as well. In the end, a web crawler may be used by anyone seeking to collect information out on the Internet.

Web crawlers may operate one time only, say for a particular one-time project. If its purpose is for something long term, as is the case with search engines, they may be programed to comb through the Internet periodically to determine whether there has been any significant changes. If a site is experiencing heavy traffic or technical difficulties, the spider may be programmed to note that and revisit the site again, hopefully after the technical issues have subsided.

Web crawling is an important method for collecting data on, and keeping up with, the rapidly expanding Internet. A vast number of web pages are continually being added every day, and information is constantly changing. A web crawler is a way for the search engines and other users to regularly ensure that their databases are up to date.

Crawler Overview

In this article, it will introduce a simple Web crawler with a simple interface, to describe the crawling story in a simple C# program. My crawler takes the input interface of any Internet navigator to simplify the process. The user just has to input the URL to be crawled in the navigation bar, and click "Go".

The crawler has a URL queue that is equivalent to the URL server in any large scale search engine. The crawler works with multiple threads to fetch URLs from the crawler queue. Then the retrieved pages are saved in a storage area as shown in the figure.

The fetched URLs are requested from the Web using a C# Sockets library to avoid locking in any other C# libraries. The retrieved pages are parsed to extract new URL references to be put in the crawler queue, again to a certain depth

Questions based on web crawling:

What is Web Crawling ? How is it useful?
Explain Web Crawling Overviews.

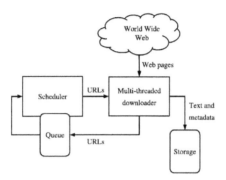

WEB INDEXING

Web indexing (or "Internet indexing") includes back-of-book-style indexes to individual websites or an intranet, and the creation of keyword metadata to provide a more useful vocabulary for Internet or onsite search engines. With the increase in the number of periodicals that have articles online, web indexing is also becoming important for periodical websites.

Back-of-the-book-style web indexes may be called "web site A-Z indexes." The implication with "A-Z" is that there is an alphabetical browse view or interface. This interface differs from that of a browse through layers of hierarchical categories (also known as a taxonomy) which are not necessarily alphabetical, but are also found on some web sites.

Web site A-Z indexes have several advantages over Search Engines - Language is full of homographs and synonyms and not all the references found will be relevant.

A human-produced index has someone check each a every part of the text to find everything relevant to the search term, while a Search Engine leaves the responsibility for finding the information with the enquirer.

Although an A-Z index could be used to index multiple sites, rather than the multiple pages of a single site, this is unusual.

Metadata web indexing involves assigning keywords or phrases to web pages or web sites within a meta-tag field, so that the web page or web site can be retrieved with a search engine that is customized to search the keywords field. This may or may not involve using keywords restricted to a controlled vocabulary list.

Questions based on web indexing:
1. Explain Web Indexing.

WEB SEARCHING

Web Searching defines searching of information on World Wide Web. The search technology uses semantic and extraction capabilities to recognize the best answer from within a sea of relevant pages.

Web Searching is done through an engine called Web Search Engine. The search results are generally presented in a list of results and are often called *hits*. The information may consist of web pages, images, information and other types of files.

Some search engines also mine data available in databases or open directories. Unlike Web directories, which are maintained by human editors, search engines operate algorithmically or are a mixture of algorithmic and human input.

Web Search Tools

Choose the Right Tool: There are three distinct types of Web search tools: Web directories, Web indexes, and specialized databases.

Browse the Best Sites: Web directories are selective. They provide short descriptions of Web sites and are a good place to start a general search or to survey what's available on a broad topic.

Search for Specific Information: Web indexes ("search engines") are huge databases containing the full text of millions of Web pages. Start here when your search is specific or well-defined. Specialized factual databases (the "invisible Web") are also good sources for answering specific questions.

Meta-Search to Save Time: A meta-searcher allows you to send one search to many different Web tools (key directories and indexes) simultaneously.

Smart Search Techniques: Use effective search techniques in all of these sources. Choose good search terms, speak the "language" of the search tool (symbols, boolean operators) and use limiting to focus search results.

SEARCH ENGINE OPTIMIZATION (SEO) AND LIMITATIONS

Search Engine Optimization (SEO)

SEO is an acronym for "search engine optimization" or "search engine optimizer." Deciding to hire an SEO is a big decision that can potentially improve your site and save time, but you can also risk damage to your site and reputation. Make sure to research the potential advantages as well as the damage that an irresponsible SEO can do to your site. Many SEOs and other agencies and consultants provide useful services for website owners, including:

- Review of your site content or structure
- Technical advice on website development: for example, hosting, redirects, error pages, use of JavaScript
- Content development
- Management of online business development campaigns
- Keyword research
- SEO training
- Expertise in specific markets and geographies.
- SEO is a key part of any web site to drive and promote traffic, and not just any traffic, the most relevant traffic possible.

Limitations

Great Expectations

Search engine optimisation features, such as those mentioned on our SEO page, will help to get your website noticed, but they won't work miracles. People with a website to advertise tend to expect too much of search engines, either through underestimating the sheer number of websites that touch on a particular topic, or through overestimating the abilities of the search engines.

They also overestimate the ability of internet users to make the most of what the search engines offer. Few users delve beyond the first couple of pages of search results, and fewer still read the search engines' guidelines to efficient searching

You should be aware that merely submitting a website to a search engine does not guarantee that the search engine will include that website in its search results. Different search engines work in different ways, with varying levels of efficiency. They also work at different speeds: some become aware of new websites almost instantly, while others may take weeks.

Ratings

Search engines, imperfect though they are, attempt to rank websites mainly according to two factors:

> relevance, which can be increased by skilled search engine optimisation, and popularity, which is largely out of the hands of the website's owner and its designer.

> Most search engines place great emphasis on the number of significant links to particular websites, and are able to detect the approximate number and quality of these links. The greater the number of relevant links, the more significant the website will appear to be.

Obviously, the number of links to your website will be largely out of your control, but there are legitimate ways to increase the number. Co-operation between websites that deal with a particular topic, in which each website includes links to the others, is one way of increasing your profile with the search engines..

The sad truth is that most new websites start near the bottom of most search engines' rankings and work their way up over time. You should be very wary of organisations claiming to guarantee that your website will instantly appear near the top of the rankings. There are many underhand ways of achieving this, and the search engines are wise to most of them. It is quite possible that your website will indeed appear near the top of the rankings, but it won't stay there for long if the wrong methods are used. Once the search engines identify fraud, they will penalise your website, and perhaps even blacklist it.

Questions based on SEO:
What is SEO? How is SEO useful in day-to-day life?
Explain the limitations of SEO.?

INTRODUCTION TO THE SEMANTIC WEB

The Semantic Web is a web that is able to describe things in a way that computers can understand.

> The Beatles was a popular band from Liverpool.
> John Lennon was a member of the Beatles.
> "Hey Jude" was recorded by the Beatles.

Sentences like the ones above can be understood by people. But how can they be understood by computers?

Statements are built with syntax rules. The syntax of a language defines the rules for building the language statements. But how can syntax become semantic?

This is what the Semantic Web is all about. Describing things in a way that computers applications can understand it.

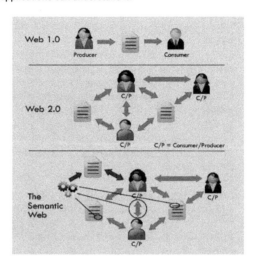

The Semantic Web is **not about links** between web pages.

The Semantic Web describes the **relationships between** things (like A is a part of B and Y is a member of Z) and the **properties of things** (like size, weight, age, and price).

"If HTML and the Web made all the online documents look like one huge **book**, RDF, schema, and inference languages will make all the data in the world look like one huge **database**"

Tim Berners-Lee, Weaving the Web, 1999

An Introduction To Social Networks

Wikipedia defines a social network service as a service which *"focuses on the building and verifying of online social networks for communities of people who share interests and activities, or who are interested in exploring the interests and activities of others, and which necessitates the use of software."*.

What Can Social Networks Be Used For?

Social networks can provide a range of benefits to members of an organisation:

Support for learning: Social networks can enhance informal learning and support social connections within groups of learners and with those involved in the support of learning.

Support for members of an organisation: Social networks can potentially be used my all members of an organisation, and not just those involved in working with students. Social networks can help the development of communities of practice.

Engaging with others: Passive use of social networks can provide valuable business intelligence and feedback on institutional services (although this may give rise to ethical concerns).

Ease of access to information and applications: The ease of use of many social networking services can provide benefits to users by simplifying access to other tools and applications. The Facebook Platform provides an example of how a social networking service can be used as an environment for other toolsCommon interface: A possible benefit of social networks may be the common interface which spans work / social boundaries. Since such services are often used in a personal capacity the interface and the way the service works may be familiar, thus minimising training and support needed to exploit the services in a professional context. This can, however, also be a barrier to those who wish to have strict boundaries between work and social activities

A report published by OCLC provides the following definition of social networking sites: "*Web sites primarily designed to facilitate interaction between users who share interests, attitudes and activities, such as Facebook, Mixi and MySpace.*"

Examples of popular social networking services include:

Facebook: Facebook is a social networking Web site that allows people to communicate with their friends and exchange information. In May 2007 Facebook launched the Facebook Platform which provides a framework for developers to create applications that interact with core Facebook features [3].

MySpace: MySpace [4] is a social networking Web site offering an interactive, user-submitted network of friends, personal profiles, blogs and groups, commonly used for sharing photos, music and videos.

Advanced Web Tehnologies

Ning: An online platform for creating social Web sites and social networks aimed at users who want to create networks around specific interests or have limited technical skills [5].

Twitter: Twitter [6] is an example of a micro-blogging service [7]. Twitter can be used in a variety of ways including sharing brief information with users and providing support for one's peers.

Opportunities And Challenges

The popularity and ease of use of social networking services have excited institutions with their potential in a variety of areas.
However effective use of social networking services poses a number of challenges for institutions including long-term sustainability of the services; user concerns over use of social tools in a work or study context; a variety of technical issues and legal issues such as copyright, privacy, accessibility.

Exercise:

Explain Semantic Web? How does it differ from Web1.0 and Web2.0?
What is search engine? Explain its working?
What is web crawler? Explain how it works?
Explain the architecture of web describing various components?
Explain the difference between website and web portal?
What is search engine optimization? State its importance?
Give the overview of different search engines?
Write a note on caching?

SERVLETS

INTRODUCTION TO SERVLETS

SERVLET: A servlet is a small Java program that runs within a Web server. Servlets receive and respond to requests from Web clients, usually across HTTP, the HyperText Transfer Protocol.

To implement this interface, you can write a generic servlet that extends javax.servlet.GenericServlet or an HTTP servlet that extends javax.servlet.http.HttpServlet.

This interface defines methods to initialize a servlet, to service requests, and to remove a servlet from the server.

What are JAVA Servlets?

A **Servlet** is a Java class which conforms to the **Java Servlet** API, a protocol by which a Java class may respond to HTTP requests. Thus, a software developer may use a servlet to add dynamic content to a Web server using the Java platform. The generated content is commonly HTML, but may be other data such as XML. Servlets are the Java counterpart to non-Java dynamic Web content technologies such as CGI and ASP.NET. Servlets can maintain state in session variables across many server transactions by using HTTP cookies, or URL rewriting.

Servlets are snippets of Java programs which run inside a

Servlet Container. A Servlet Container is much like a Web Server which handles user requests and generates responses. Servlet Container is different from a Web Server because it can not only serve requests for static content like HTML page, GIF images, etc., it can also contain Java Servlets and JSP pages to generate dynamic response. Servlet Container is responsible for loading and maintaining the lifecycle of the a Java Servlet. Servlet Container can be used standalone or more often used in conjunction with a Web server. Example of a Servlet Container is Tomcat and that of Web Server is Apache.

Servlets vs CGI

The traditional way of adding functionality to a Web Server is the Common Gateway Interface (CGI), a language-independent interface that allows a server to start an external process which gets information about a request through environment variables, the command line and its standard input stream and writes response data to its standard output stream. Each request is answered in a separate process by a separate instance of the CGI program, or CGI script (as it is often called because CGI programs are usually written in interpreted languages like Perl).

Servlets have several advantages over CGI

A Servlet does not run in a separate process. This removes the overhead of creating a new process for each request.
A Servlet stays in memory between requests. A CGI program
(and probably also an extensive runtime system or interpreter) needs to be loaded and started for each CGI request.
There is only a single instance which answers all requests concurrently. This saves memory and allows a Servlet to easily manage persistent data.

SERVLET LIFE CYCLE

The servlet lifecycle consists of the following steps

The servlet class is loaded by the Web container during start-up.
The Web container calls the init() method. This method initializes the servlet and must be called before the servlet can service any requests. In the entire life of a servlet, the init() method is called only once.
After initialization, the servlet can service client requests. Each request is serviced in its own separate thread. The Web container calls the service() method of the servlet for every request. The service() method determines the kind of request being made and dispatches it to an appropriate method to handle the request. The developer of the servlet must provide an implementation for these methods. If a request for a method that is not implemented by the servlet is made, the method of the parent class is called, typically resulting in an error being returned to the requester.
Finally, the Web container calls the destroy() method that takes the servlet out of service. The destroy() method, like init(), is called only once in the lifecycle of a servlet.

Here is a simple servlet that just generates HTML. Note that HttpServlet is a subclass of GenericServlet, an implementation of the Servlet interface. The service() method dispatches requests to methods doGet(), doPost(), doPut(), doDelete(), etc., according to the HTTP request.

LIFECYCLE:

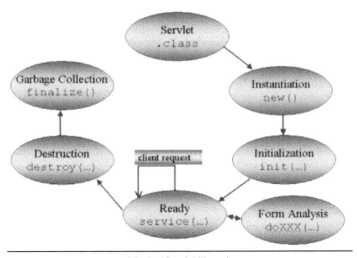

A typical Servlet lifecycle

The Basic Servlet Architecture

A Servlet, in its most general form, is an instance of a class which implements the javax.servlet.Servlet interface. Most Servlets, however, extend one of the standard implementations of that interface, namely javax.servlet.GenericServlet and javax.servlet.http.HttpServlet. In this tutorial we'll be discussing only HTTP Servlets which extend the javax.servlet.http.HttpServlet class.

In order to initialize a Servlet, a server application loads the Servlet class (and probably other classes which are referenced by the Servlet) and creates an instance by calling the no-args constructor. Then it calls the Servlet's init(ServletConfig config) method. The Servlet should perform one-time setup procedures in this method and store the ServletConfig object so that it can be retrieved later by calling the Servlet's getServletConfig() method. This is handled by GenericServlet.
Servlets which extend GenericServlet (or its subclass HttpServlet) should call super.init(config) at the beginning of the init method to make use of this feature. The ServletConfig object contains Servlet parameters and a reference to the Servlet's

ServletContext. The init method is guaranteed to be called only once during the Servlet's lifecycle. It does not need to be thread-safe because the service method will not be called until the call to init returns.

When the Servlet is initialized, its service(ServletRequest req, ServletResponse res) method is called for every request to the Servlet. The method is called concurrently (i.e. multiple threads may call this method at the same time) so it should be implemented in a thread-safe manner. Techniques for ensuring that the service method is not called concurrently, for the cases where this is not possible.

When the Servlet needs to be unloaded (e.g. because a new version should be loaded or the server is shutting down) the destroy() method is called. There may still be threads that execute the service method when destroy is called, so destroy has to be thread-safe. All resources which were allocated in init should be released in destroy. This method is guaranteed to be called only once during the Servlet's lifecycle.

```java
import java.io.IOException;
import java.io.PrintWriter;
import javax.servlet.ServletException;
import javax.servlet.http.HttpServlet;
import javax.servlet.http.HttpServletRequest;
import javax.servlet.http.HttpServletResponse;

public class HelloWorld extends HttpServlet
{
  Public void doGet(HttpServletRequest request, HttpServletResponse response)
    throws ServletException, IOException
    {
    PrintWriter out = response.getWriter();
    out.println("<!DOCTYPE HTML PUBLIC \"-//W3C//DTD HTML
          4.0 " + "Transitional//EN\">\n" + "<html>\n" +
          "<head><title>Hello WWW</title></head>\n" +
          "<body>\n" + "<h1>Hello WWW</h1>\n" +
          "</body></html>");
    }
}
```

SERVLET CLASSES

Servlets are actually simple Java classes which must implement the javax.servlet.Servlet interface. This interface contains a total of five methods. javax.servlet package already provides two classes which implement this interface i.e. GenericServlet and HttpServlet. So all we need to do is to extend one of these classes and override the method(s) you need for your Servlet.

GenericServlet is a very simple class which only implements the *javax.servlet.Servlet* interface and provides only basic functionality. On the other hand, HttpServlet is a more useful class which provides methods to work with the HTTP protocol. So if your Servlet works with HTTP protocol (in most cases this will be the case) then you *should* extend javax.servlet.http.HttpServlet class to build Servlets and this is what I am going to do in this topic.

Servlets once initialized are kept in memory. So every request which the Servlet Container receives, is delegated to the in-memory Java Servlet which then generates the response. This 'kept in memory' feature makes Java Servlets, a fast and efficient method of building web applications.

SERVLET

A Servlet is an object that receives a request and generates a response based on that request. The basic servlet package defines Java objects to represent servlet requests and responses, as well as objects to reflect the servlet's configuration parameters and execution environment. The package javax.servlet.http defines HTTP-specific subclasses of the generic servlet elements, including session management objects that track multiple requests and responses between the Web server and a client. Servlets may be packaged in a WAR file as a Web application.

Servlets can be generated automatically by JavaServer Pages (JSP) compiler, or alternately use template engines such as WebMacro or Apache Velocity to generate HTML. Often servlets are used in conjunction with JSPs in a pattern called "Model 2", which is a flavor of the model-view-controller pattern.

SERVLET REQUEST

This interface is for getting data from the client to the servlet for a service request. Network service developers implement the ServletRequest interface. The methods are then used by servlets when the service method is executed; the ServletRequest object is passed as an argument to the service method.

Some of the data provided by the ServletRequest object includes parameter names and values, attributes, and an input stream. Subclasses of ServletRequest can provide additional protocol-specific data. For example, HTTP data is provided by the interface HttpServletRequest, which extends ServletRequest. This framework provides the servlet's only access to this data.

getAttribute
public abstract Object getAttribute(String name)
Returns the value of the named attribute of the request, or null if the attribute does not exist. This method allows access to request information not already provided by the other methods in this interface. Attribute names should follow the same convention as package names. The following predefined attributes are provided.

Attribute Name	Attribute Type	Description
javax.net.ssl.	String	The string name of the SSL cipher
peer_certificates	Certificate	which authenticates the client. This cert.X509is only available when SSL is usedwith client authentication is used.
javax.net.ssl.	Array	of the chain of X.509 certificates
ssl.session	SSLSession	An SSL session object, if the request was made using SSL

The package (and hence attribute) names beginning with java.*, and javax.* are reserved for use by Javasoft. Similarly, com.sun.* is reserved for use by Sun Microsystems.
Parameters:
name - the name of the attribute whose value is required

getAttributeNames
public abstract Enumeration getAttributeNames()
Returns an enumeration of attribute names contained in this request.

getCharacterEncoding
public abstract String getCharacterEncoding()
Returns the character set encoding for the input of this request.

getContentLength
public abstract int getContentLength()
Returns the size of the request entity data, or -1 if not known. Same as the CGI variable CONTENT_LENGTH.

getContentType
public abstract String getContentType()
Returns the Internet Media Type of the request entity data, or null if not known. Same as the CGI variable CONTENT_TYPE.

getInputStream
public abstract ServletInputStream getInputStream() throws IOException Returns an input stream for reading binary data in the request body.
Throws: IllegalStateException
        if getReader has been called on this same request.
Throws: IOException
        on other I/O related errors.
See Also:
        getReader

getParameter
public abstract String getParameter(String name)
Returns a string containing the lone value of the specified parameter, or null if the parameter does not exist. For example, in an HTTP servlet this method would

return the value of the specified query string parameter. Servlet writers should use this method only when they are sure that there is only one value for the parameter. If the parameter has (or could have) multiple values, servlet writers should use getParameterValues. If a multiple valued parameter name is passed as an argument, the return value is implementation dependent.
Parameters:
name - the name of the parameter whose value is required.

getParameterNames
public abstract Enumeration getParameterNames()
Returns the parameter names for this request as an enumeration of strings, or an empty enumeration if there are no parameters or the input stream is empty. The input stream would be empty if all the data had been read from the stream returned by the method getInputStream.

getParameterValues
public abstract String[] getParameterValues(String name)
Returns the values of the specified parameter for the request as an array of strings, or null if the named parameter does not exist.
For example, in an HTTP servlet this method would return the values of the specified query string or posted form as an array of strings.
Parameters:
name - the name of the parameter whose value is required.

getProtocol
public abstract String getProtocol()
Returns the protocol and version of the request as a string of the form <protocol>/<major version>.<minor version>. Same as the CGI variable SERVER_PROTOCOL.

getScheme
public abstract String getScheme()
Returns the scheme of the URL used in this request, for example "http", "https", or "ftp". Different schemes have different rules for constructing URLs, as noted in RFC 1738. The URL used to create a request may be reconstructed using this scheme, the server name and port, and additional information such as URIs.

getServerName
public abstract String getServerName()
Returns the host name of the server that received the request.
Same as the CGI variable SERVER_NAME.

getServerPort
public abstract int getServerPort()
Returns the port number on which this request was received. Same as the CGI variable SERVER_PORT.

getReader
public abstract BufferedReader getReader() throws IOException

Returns a buffered reader for reading text in the request body. This translates character set encodings as appropriate.

Throws: UnsupportedEncodingException

if the character set encoding is unsupported, so the text can't be correctly decoded.

Throws: IllegalStateException if getInputStream has been called on this same request.

Throws: IOException on other I/O related errors.

getRemoteAddr
public abstract String getRemoteAddr()

Returns the IP address of the agent that sent the request. Same as the CGI variable REMOTE_ADDR.

getRemoteHost
public abstract String getRemoteHost()

Returns the fully qualified host name of the agent that sent the request. Same as the CGI variable REMOTE_HOST.

setAttribute
public abstract void setAttribute (String key, Object o)

This method stores an attribute in the request context; these attributes will be reset between requests. Attribute names should follow the same convention as package names.

The package (and hence attribute) names beginning with java.*, and javax.* are reserved for use by Javasoft. Similarly, com.sun.* is reserved for use by Sun Microsystems.

Parameters:

key - a String specifying the name of the attribute

o - a context object stored with the key.

Throws: IllegalStateException if the named attribute already has a value.

getRealPath
public abstract String getRealPath(String path)

getRealPath() is deprecated. *This method has been deprecated in preference to the same method found in the ServletContext interface.*

Applies alias rules to the specified virtual path and returns the corresponding real path, or null if the translation can not be performed for any reason. For example, an HTTP servlet would resolve the path using the virtual docroot, if virtual hosting is enabled, and with the default docroot otherwise. Calling this method with the string "/" as an argument returns the document root.

Parameters:

path - the virtual path to be translated to a real path

SERVLET RESPONSE:

Defines an object to assist a servlet in sending a response to the client. The servlet container creates a ServletResponse object and passes it as an argument to the servlet's service method.

To send binary data in a MIME body response, use the ServletOutputStream returned by getOutputStream(). To send character data, use the PrintWriter object returned by getWriter(). To mix binary and text data, for example, to create a multipart response, use a ServletOutputStream and manage the character sections manually.

The charset for the MIME body response can be specified with setContentType(java.lang.String). For example, "text/html; charset=Shift_JIS". The charset can alternately be set using setLocale(java.util.Locale). If no charset is specified, ISO-8859-1 will be used. The setContentType or setLocale method must be called before getWriter for the charset to affect the construction of the writer.

Various methods used and in detail:

getCharacterEncoding
public java.lang.String getCharacterEncoding()
Returns the name of the charset used for the MIME body sent in this response.
If no charset has been assigned, it is implicitly set to ISO-8859-1 (Latin-1).
See RFC 2047 (http://ds.internic.net/rfc/rfc2045.txt) for more information about character encoding and MIME.
Returns:
a String specifying the name of the charset, for example,
ISO-8859-1

getOutputStream
public ServletOutputStream getOutputStream() throws java.io.IOException
Returns a ServletOutputStream suitable for writing binary data in the response. The servlet container does not encode the binary data.
Calling flush() on the ServletOutputStream commits the response. Either this method or getWriter() may be called to write the body, not both.
Returns:
a ServletOutputStream for writing binary data
Throws:
IllegalStateException - if the getWriter method has been called on this response
java.io.IOException - if an input or output exception occurred

getWriter
public java.io.PrintWriter getWriter() throws java.io.IOException
Returns a PrintWriter object that can send character text to the client. The

Advanced Web Tehnologies

character encoding used is the one specified in the charset= property of the setContentType(java.lang.String) method, which must be called *before* calling this method for the charset to take effect.

If necessary, the MIME type of the response is modified to reflect the character encoding used.

Calling flush() on the PrintWriter commits the response.

Either this method or getOutputStream() may be called to write the body, not both.

Returns:

a PrintWriter object that can return character data to the client

Throws:

java.io.UnsupportedEncodingException - if the charset specified in

setContentType cannot be used

IllegalStateException - if the getOutputStream method has already been called

for this response object

java.io.IOException - if an input or output exception occurred

setContentLength

public void **setContentLength**(int len)

Sets the length of the content body in the response In HTTP servlets, this method sets the HTTP Content-Length header.

Parameters:

len - an integer specifying the length of the content being returned to the client;

sets the Content-Length header

setContentType

public void **setContentType**(java.lang.String type)

Sets the content type of the response being sent to the client. The content type may include the type of character encoding used, for example, text/html; charset=ISO-8859-4.

If obtaining a PrintWriter, this method should be called first.

Parameters:

type - a String specifying the MIME type of the content

setBufferSize

public void **setBufferSize**(int size)

Sets the preferred buffer size for the body of the response. The servlet container will use a buffer at least as large as the size requested. The actual buffer size used can be found using getBufferSize.

A larger buffer allows more content to be written before anything is actually sent, thus providing the servlet with more time to set appropriate status codes and headers. A smaller buffer decreases server memory load and allows the client to start receiving data more quickly.

This method must be called before any response body content is written; if content has been written, this method throws an IllegalStateException.
Parameters:
size - the preferred buffer size
Throws:
IllegalStateException - if this method is called after content has been written

getBufferSize
public int getBufferSize()
Returns the actual buffer size used for the response. If no buffering is used, this method returns 0.
Returns:
the actual buffer size used

flushBuffer
public void flushBuffer() throws java.io.IOException
Forces any content in the buffer to be written to the client. A call to this method automatically commits the response, meaning the status code and headers will be written.

resetBuffer
public void resetBuffer()
Clears the content of the underlying buffer in the response without clearing headers or status code. If the response has been committed, this method throws an IllegalStateException.
Since: 2.3

isCommitted
public boolean isCommitted()
Returns a boolean indicating if the response has been committed. A commited response has already had its status code and headers written.
Returns: a boolean indicating if the response has been committed

reset
public void reset()
Clears any data that exists in the buffer as well as the status code and headers. If the response has been committed, this method throws an IllegalStateException.
Throws:
IllegalStateException - if the response has already been committed

setLocale
public void setLocale(java.util.Locale loc)
Sets the locale of the response, setting the headers

(including the Content-Type's charset) as appropriate. This method should be called before a call to getWriter(). By default, the response locale is the default locale for the server.
Parameters:
loc - the locale of the response

getLocale
public java.util.Locale getLocale()
Returns the locale assigned to the response.

SERVLETCONTEXT

Defines a set of methods that a servlet uses to communicate with its servlet container, for example, to get the MIME type of a file, dispatch requests, or write to a log file.

There is one context per "web application" per Java Virtual Machine. (A "web application" is a collection of servlets and content installed under a specific subset of the server's URL namespace such as /catalog and possibly installed via a .war file.)

In the case of a web application marked "distributed" in its deployment descriptor, there will be one context instance for each virtual machine. In this situation, the context cannot be used as a location to share global information (because the information won't be truly global). Use an external resource like a database instead.

The ServletContext object is contained within the ServletConfig object, which the Web server provides the servlet when the servlet is initialized.

Methods and details used in details:

getContext
public ServletContext getContext(java.lang.String uripath)
Returns a ServletContext object that corresponds to a specified URL on the server.
This method allows servlets to gain access to the context for various parts of the server, and as needed obtain RequestDispatcher objects from the context. The given path must be begin with "/", is interpreted relative to the server's document root and is matched against the context roots of other web applications hosted on this container.
In a security conscious environment, the servlet container may return null for a given URL.
Parameters:
uripath - a String specifying the context path of another web application in the container.

Returns:
the ServletContext object that corresponds to the named URL, or null if either none exists or the container wishes to restrict this access.

getMajorVersion
public int **getMajorVersion**()
Returns the major version of the Java Servlet API that this servlet container supports. All implementations that comply with
Version 2.3 must have this method return the integer 2.
Returns: 2

getMinorVersion
public int **getMinorVersion**()
Returns the minor version of the Servlet API that this servlet container supports. All implementations that comply with Version 2.3 must have this method return the integer 3.
Returns: 3

getMimeType
public java.lang.String **getMimeType**(java.lang.String file)
Returns the MIME type of the specified file, or null if the
> MIME type is not known. The MIME type is determined by the configuration of the servlet container, and may be specified in a web application deployment descriptor.
> Common MIME types are "text/html" and "image/gif".

Parameters:
file - a String specifying the name of a file
Returns:
a String specifying the file's MIME type

getResourcePaths
public java.util.Set **getResourcePaths**(java.lang.String path)
Returns a directory-like listing of all the paths to resources
within the web application whose longest sub-path matches the supplied path argument. Paths indicating subdirectory paths end with a '/'. The returned paths are all relative to the root of the web application and have a leading '/'. For example, for a web application containing

/welcome.html
/catalog/index.html
/catalog/products.html
/catalog/offers/books.html
/catalog/offers/music.html
/customer/login.jsp
/WEB-INF/web.xml
/WEB-INF/classes/com.acme.OrderServlet.class,

getResourcePaths("/") returns {"/welcome.html", "/catalog/", "/customer/", "/WEB-INF/"}
getResourcePaths("/catalog/")
returns {"/catalog/index.html","/catalog/products.html", "/catalog/offers/"}.
Parameters:
the - partial path used to match the resources, which must start with a /
Returns:
a Set containing the directory listing, or null if there are no resources in the web application whose path begins with the supplied path.
Since:
Servlet 2.3

getResource
public java.net.URL **getResource**(java.lang.String path) throws
java.net.MalformedURLException
Returns a URL to the resource that is mapped to a specified path. The path must begin with a "/" and is interpreted as relative to the current context root.

This method allows the servlet container to make a resource available to servlets from any source. Resources can be located on a local or remote file system, in a database, or in a .war file.

The servlet container must implement the URL handlers and URLConnection objects that are necessary to access the resource.

This method returns null if no resource is mapped to the pathname.

Some containers may allow writing to the URL returned by this method using the methods of the URL class.

The resource content is returned directly, so be aware that requesting a .jsp page returns the JSP source code. Use a RequestDispatcher instead to include results of an execution.

This method has a different purpose than java.lang.Class.getResource, which looks up resources based on a class loader. This method does not use class loaders.
Parameters:
path - a String specifying the path to the resource
Returns:
the resource located at the named path, or null if there is no resource at that path
Throws:
java.net.MalformedURLException - if the pathname is not given in the correct form

getResourceAsStream
publicjava.io.InputStream

getResourceAsStream(java.lang.String path)
Returns the resource located at the named path as an
InputStream object.
The data in the InputStream can be of any type or length. The path must be
specified according to the rules given in getResource. This method returns null if no
resource exists at the specified path.

Meta-information such as content length and content type that is available via
getResource method is lost when using this method.

The servlet container must implement the URL handlers and URLConnection
objects necessary to access the resource.

This method is different from java.lang. Class. Get Resource As Stream, which
uses a class loader. This method allows servlet containers to make a resource
available to a servlet from any location, without using a class loader.
Parameters:
name - a String specifying the path to the resource
Returns:
the InputStream returned to the servlet, or null if no resource exists at the
specified path

getRequestDispatcher
public RequestDispatcher getRequestDispatcher(java.lang.String path)
Returns a RequestDispatcher object that acts as a wrapper for the resource
located at the given path. A RequestDispatcher object can be used to forward a
request to the resource or to include the resource in a response. The resource
can be dynamic or static.
The pathname must begin with a "/" and is interpreted as relative to the current
context root. Use getContext to obtain a RequestDispatcher for resources in foreign
contexts. This method returns null if the ServletContext cannot return a
RequestDispatcher.
Parameters:
path - a String specifying the pathname to the resource
Returns:
a RequestDispatcher object that acts as a wrapper for the resource at the
specified path

See Also:
RequestDispatcher, getContext(java.lang.String)

getNamedDispatcher
public   RequestDispatcher
getNamedDispatcher(java.lang.String name)
Returns a RequestDispatcher object that acts as a wrapper for the named servlet.
Servlets (and JSP pages also) may be given names via server administration or
via a web application deployment descriptor. A servlet instance can determine its

name using ServletConfig.getServletName().
This method returns null if the ServletContext cannot return a Request Dispatcher for any reason.
Parameters:
name - a String specifying the name of a servlet to wrap
Returns:
a RequestDispatcher object that acts as a wrapper for the named servlet

THREADING MODELS

In computer science, the term **threaded code** refers to a compiler implementation technique where the generated code has a form that essentially consists entirely of calls to subroutines. The code may be processed by an interpreter, or may simply be a sequence of machine code call instructions.

One of the main advantages of threaded code is that it is very compact, compared to code generated by alternative code generation techniques and alternative calling conventions. This advantage usually comes at the expense of slightly slower execution speed (usually just a single machine instruction). However, sometimes there is a synergistic effect —sometimes more compact code is smaller *and* significantly faster than non-threaded code.[1] A program small enough to fit entirely in a computer processor's cache may run faster than a less-compact program that suffers constant cache misses.

HTTPSESSION

public interface HttpSession
Provides a way to identify a user across more than one page request or visit to a Web site and to store information about that user.
The servlet container uses this interface to create a session between an HTTP client and an HTTP server. The session persists for a specified time period, across more than one connection or page request from the user. A session usually corresponds to one user, who may visit a site many times. The server can maintain a session in many ways such as using cookies or rewriting URLs.
This interface allows servlets to

   View and manipulate information about a session, such as the session identifier, creation time, and last accessed time

   Bind objects to sessions, allowing user information to persist across multiple user connections

When an application stores an object in or removes an object from a session, the session checks whether the object implements HttpSessionBindingListener. If it

Advanced Web Tehnologies

does, the servlet notifies the object that it has been bound to or unbound from the session.

A servlet should be able to handle cases in which the client does not choose to join a session, such as when cookies are intentionally turned off. Until the client joins the session, isNew returns true. If the client chooses not to join the session, getSession will return a different session on each request, and isNew will always return true.

Session information is scoped only to the current web application (ServletContext), so information stored in one context will not be directly visible in another.

Methods used in detail:

getCreationTime
public long **getCreationTime**()
> Returns the time when this session was created, measured in milliseconds since midnight January 1, 1970 GMT.

Returns:
a long specifying when this session was created, expressed in milliseconds since 1/1/1970 GMT

Throws:
java.lang.IllegalStateException - if this method is called on an invalidated session

getId
public java.lang.String **getId**()
Returns a string containing the unique identifier assigned to this session. The identifier is assigned by the servlet container and is implementation dependent.
Returns:
a string specifying the identifier assigned to this session

getLastAccessedTime
public long **getLastAccessedTime**()
Returns the last time the client sent a request associated with this session, as the number of milliseconds since midnight January 1, 1970 GMT.
Actions that your application takes, such as getting or setting a value associated with the session, do not affect the access time.
Returns:
a long representing the last time the client sent a request associated with this session, expressed in milliseconds since 1/1/1970 GMT

setMaxInactiveInterval
public void **setMaxInactiveInterval**(int interval)
Specifies the time, in seconds, between client requests before the servlet

container will invalidate this session. A negative time indicates the session should never timeout.
Parameters:
interval - An integer specifying the number of seconds

getMaxInactiveInterval
public int **getMaxInactiveInterval**()
Returns the maximum time interval, in seconds, that the servlet container will keep this session open between client accesses. After this interval, the servlet container will invalidate the session. The maximum time interval can be set with the setMaxInactiveInterval method. A negative time indicates the session should never timeout.
Returns:
an integer specifying the number of seconds this session remains open between client requests

getSessionContext
public HttpSessionContext **getSessionContext**()
Deprecated. *As of Version 2.1, this method is deprecated and has no replacement. It will be removed in a future version of the Java Servlet API.*

getAttribute
public java.lang.Object **getAttribute**(java.lang.String name) Returns the object bound with the specified name in this session, or null if no object is bound under the name.
Parameters:
name - a string specifying the name of the object
Returns:
the object with the specified name
Throws:
java.lang.IllegalStateException - if this method is called on an invalidated session

getValue
public java.lang.Object **getValue**(java.lang.String name)
Deprecated. *As of Version 2.2, this method is replaced by getAttribute(java.lang.String).*
Parameters:
name - a string specifying the name of the object
Returns:
the object with the specified name
Throws:
java.lang.IllegalStateException - if this method is called on an invalidated session

getAttributeNames
public java.util.Enumeration **getAttributeNames**()
Returns an Enumeration of String objects containing the names of all the objects
bound to this session.
Returns:
an Enumeration of String objects specifying the names of all the objects bound
to this session
Throws:
java.lang.IllegalStateException - if this method is called on an invalidated session

getValueNames
public java.lang.String[] **getValueNames**()
Deprecated. *As of Version 2.2, this method is replaced by getAttributeNames()*
Returns:
an array of String objects specifying the names of all the objects bound to this
session
Throws:
java.lang.IllegalStateException - if this method is called on an invalidated session

setAttribute
public void **setAttribute**(java.lang.String name, java.lang.Object value)
Binds an object to this session, using the name specified. If an object of the
same name is already bound to the session, the object is replaced.
After this method executes, and if the object implements Http
Session Binding Listener, the container calls Http Session Binding Listener.value
Bound.
Parameters:
name - the name to which the object is bound; cannot be null
value - the object to be bound; cannot be null
Throws:
java.lang.IllegalStateException - if this method is called on an invalidated session

putValue
public void putValue(java.lang.String name, java.lang.Object value)
Deprecated. *As   of   Version   2.2,   this   method   is   replaced   by*
setAttribute(java.lang.String, java.lang.Object)
Parameters:
name - the name to which the object is bound; cannot be null
value - the object to be bound; cannot be null
Throws:
java.lang.IllegalStateException - if this method is called on an invalidated session

removeAttribute
public void **removeAttribute**(java.lang.String name)

Removes the object bound with the specified name from this session. If the session does not have an object bound with the specified name, this method does nothing.

After this method executes, and if the object implements Http Session Binding Listener, the container calls Http Session Binding Listener. value Unbound.

Parameters:
name - the name of the object to remove from this session
Throws:
java.lang.IllegalStateException - if this method is called on an invalidated session

removeValue
public void **removeValue**(java.lang.String name)
Deprecated. *As of Version 2.2, this method is replaced by setAttribute(java.lang.String, java.lang.Object)*
Parameters:
name - the name of the object to remove from this session
Throws:
java.lang.IllegalStateException - if this method is called on an invalidated session

invalidate
public void **invalidate**()
Invalidates this session and unbinds any objects bound to it.
Throws:
java.lang.IllegalStateException - if this method is called on an already invalidated session

isNew
public boolean **isNew**()
Returns true if the client does not yet know about the session or if the client chooses not to join the session. For example, if the server used only cookie-based sessions, and the client had disabled the use of cookies, then a session would be new on each request.
Returns:
true if the server has created a session, but the client has not yet joined
Throws:
java.lang.IllegalStateException - if this method is called on an already invalidated session

3

JAVA SERVER PAGES

JSP: JSP Development Model, Components of JSP page, Request dispatching, Session and Thread Management Java Server Pages (JSP) are an afterbirth of Java Servlets. When Java Servlets were introduced it opened many avenues to a Java programmer. Java became a full fledged application server programming language.Though Java Servlets were great, it posed one great problem.

What is the need for JSP?

If you are a programmer or a web designer you will agree with me that not every programmer is a good designer and not every good designer is a good programmer. This is the exact problem posed by Java Servlets. Which means Java Servlets required the Java programmer to know the designing skills because the Java Servlets did not separate the Programming logic from the presentation layer.

Therefore there was a need to separate the design aspects from the Core Java programmers. This was the reason why, JSP was introduced.

How does JSP solve this problem?

Java Server Pages or JSP solved just this issue. It separated the designing issues from the programming logic. Simply put, if a company were to design a JSP based website, it would first design the layout using a professional web designer. This design can then be passed onto the JSP programmer who can then insert Java code (JSP code) inside these HTML pages. Once inserted, this pure HTML pages becomes a JSP page. It is as simple as that. To give more re-usability and to further separate the programming logic Java Beans can be used. The 'usebean' property of a JSP page can just use these Java beans which is nothing but a Java class and then use the bean's methods from inside the JSP page making the JSP page very powerful. The Java bean on the other hand handle issues like connecting to the database, or making another HTTP connection etc.

Having understood the basics of a JSP page, it is then necessary to understand how to get started with JSP.

Advanced Web Tehnologies

JSP DEVELOPMENT MODEL

JSP provides a declarative, presentation-centric method of developing servlets. JSP specification itself is defined as a standard extension on top the Servlet API.

The early JSP specifications advocated two philosophical development models:

Model 1 architecture
Model 2 architecture

The 2 approaches differ essentially in the location at which the bulk of the request processing was performed.

Model 1 architecture

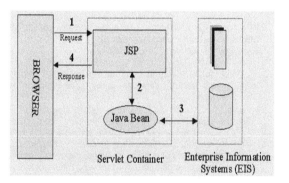

In the Model 1 architecture, the incoming request from a web browser is sent directly to the JSP page, which is responsible for processing it and replying back to the client. There is still separation of presentation from content, because all data access is performed using beans.

Model 1 architecture is suitable for simple applications. It may not be desirable for complex implementations. Indiscriminate usage of this architecture usually leads to a significant amount of scriptlets i.e. Java code embedded within the JSP page.

Another downside of this architecture is that each of the JSP pages must be individually responsible for managing application state and verifying authentication and security.

Model 2 architecture

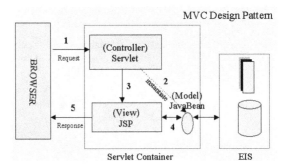

The Model 2 architecture is a server-side implementation of the popular Model/View/Controller design pattern.
Here, the processing is divided between:

> **Presentation components**: They are JSP pages that generate the HTML/XML response that determines the user interface when rendered by the browser.

> **Front components**: They are the controllers. They do not handle any presentation issues, but rather, process all the HTTP requests. Here, they are responsible for creating any beans or objects used by the presentation components, as well as deciding, depending on the user's actions, which presentation component to forward the request to. Front components can be implemented as either a servlet or JSP page.

There is no processing logic within the presentation component itself; it is simply responsible for retrieving any objects or beans that may have been previously created by the controller, and extracting the dynamic content within for insertion within its static templates.
It cleanly separates the roles and responsibilities of the developers and page designers on the programming team.

The front components present a single point of entry into the application, thus making the management of application state, security, and presentation uniform and easier to maintain.

Advanced Web Tehnologies

COMPONENTS OF JSP PAGE :

A JSP page typically contains the following components:

- Directives
- Declarations
- Expressions
- Scriptlets
- Comments

Directives
JSP directives are messages for the JSP engine. They do not directly produce any visible output, but tell the engine what to do with the rest of the JSP page.

JSP directives are always enclosed within the <%@ ... %> tag.

The two primary directives are page and include. (Note that JSP 1.1 also provides the taglib directive, which can be used for working with custom tag libraries)

Page Directive
Typically, the page directive is found at the top of almost all of your JSP pages.

There can be any number of page directives within a JSP page, although the attribute/value pair must be unique. Unrecognized attributes or values result in a translation error.

For example,

<%@ page import="java.util.*, com.foo.*" buffer="16k" %>

Include Directive
The include directive lets you separate your content into more manageable elements, such as those for including a common page header or footer.

The page included can be a static HTML page or more JSP content.

For example, the directive:

<%@ include file="copyright.html" %>

It can be used to include the contents of the indicated file at any location within the JSP page.

Declarations
JSP declarations let you define page-level variables to save information or define supporting methods that the rest of a JSP page may need.

Note that too much of declarations would turn out to be a maintenance nightmare. For that reason, and to improve reusability, it is best that logic-intensive processing is encapsulated as JavaBean components.

Declarations are found within the <%! ... %> tag.

Always end variable declarations with a semicolon, as any content must be valid Java statement.

```
<%! int i=0; %>
```
You can also declare methods. For example, you can override the initialization event in the JSP life cycle by declaring:
```
<%! public void jspInit()
        {
        //some initialization code
        }
%>
```

Expressions
The results of evaluating the expression are converted to a string and directly included within the output page.

Typically expressions are used to display simple values of variables or return values by invoking a bean's getter methods.

JSP expressions begin within `<%= ... %>` tags and do not include semicolons:
```
<%= fooVariable %>
<%= fooBean.getName() %>
```

Scriptlets
Scriptlets are embedded within `<% ... %>` tags. This code is run when the request is serviced by the JSP page. You can have just about any valid Java code within a scriptlet, and is not limited to one line of source code.

Following example combines both expressions and scriptlets:
```
<%   for   (int   i=1;   i<=4;   i++)   {   %>
   <H<%=i%>>Hello</H<%=i%>>
<% } %>
```

Comments
You can include HTML comments in JSP pages. But users can view these if they view the page's source. If you don't want users to see your comments, embed them within the `<%-- ... --%>` tag:
```
<%-- comment for server side only --%>
```

A most useful feature of JSP comments is that they can be used to selectively block out scriptlets or tags from compilation. Thus, they can play a significant role during the debugging and testing process.

Note that there are some objects are implicitly available within a JSP page. They can be used within scriptlets and expressions, without the page author first having to create them. These objects act as wrappers around underlying Java classes or interfaces typically defined within the Servlet API. The nine implicit objects:

request: represents the HttpServletRequest triggering the service invocation. Request scope.

response: represents HttpServletResponse to the request. Not used often by page authors. Page scope.

pageContext: encapsulates implementation-dependent features in PageContext. Page scope.

application: represents the ServletContext obtained from servlet configuration object. Application scope.

out: a JspWriter object that writes into the output stream. Page scope.

config: represents the ServletConfig for the JSP. Page scope.

page: synonym for the "this" operator, as an HttpJspPage. Not used often by page authors. Page scope.

session: An HttpSession. Session scope. More on sessions shortly.

exception: the uncaught Throwable object that resulted in the error page being invoked. Page scope.

Note that these implicit objects are only visible within the system generated _jspService() method. They are not visible within methods you define yourself in declarations.

REQUEST DISPATCHING

A RequestDispatcher object can forward a client's request to a resource or include the resource itself in the response back to the client. A resource can be another servlet, or an HTML file, or a JSP file, etc.

RequestDispatcher acts as an object as a wrapper for the resource located at a given path that is supplied as an argument to the getRequestDispatcher method.

For constructing a RequestDispatcher object, you can use either the ServletRequest.getRequestDispatcher() method or the ServletContext.getRequestDispatcher() method. They both do the same thing, but impose slightly different constraints on the argument path. For the former, it looks for the resource in the same webapp to which the invoking servlet belongs and the pathname specified can be relative to invoking servlet. For the latter, the pathname must begin with '/' and is interpreted relative to the root of the webapp.

To illustrate, suppose you want Servlet_A to invoke Servlet_B. If they are both in the same directory, you could accomplish this by incorporating the following code fragment in either the service method or the doGet method of Servlet_A:

```
RequestDispatcher    dispatcher = getRequest Dispatcher ("Servlet_B");
dispatcher.forward ( request, response );
```

where request, of type HttpServletRequest, is the first parameter of the enclosing service method (or the doGet method) and response, of type HttpServletResponse, the second. You could accomplish the same by

Request Dispatcher dispatcher = get Servlet Context().get Request Dispatcher("/servlet/Servlet_B");
dispatcher.forward(request, response);

The request dispatching functionality allows a servlet to delegate request handling to other components on the server. A servlet can either forward an entire request to another servlet or include bits of content from other components in its own output. In either case, this is done with a RequestDispatcher object that is obtained from the ServletContext with its new getRequestDispatcher() method. When you call this method, you specify the path to the servlet to which you are dispatching the request.

When you dispatch a request, you can set request attributes using the setAttribute() method of ServletRequest and read them using the getAttribute() method. A list of available attributes is returned by getAttributeNames().

RequestDispatcher provides two methods for dispatching requests:

forward
void **forward** (Servlet Request request, Servlet Response response) throws ServletException,IOException

Forwards a request from a servlet to another resource (servlet, JSP file, or HTML file) on the server. This method allows one servlet to do preliminary processing of a request and another resource to generate the response.

For a RequestDispatcher obtained via getRequestDispatcher(), the ServletRequest object has its path elements and parameters adjusted to match the path of the target resource.forward should be called before the response has been committed to the client. If the response already has been committed, this method throws an IllegalStateException.
Uncommitted output in the response buffer is automatically cleared before the forward.
Parameters:
request - a ServletRequest object that represents the request the client makes of the servlet

response - a ServletResponse object that represents the response the servlet returns to the client
Throws:
ServletException - if the target resource throws this exception IOException

- if the target resource throws this exception IllegalStateException - if the response was already committed.

include
    void include(ServletRequest request,ServletResponse response) throws ServletException,IOException

It includes the content of a resource (servlet, JSP page, HTML file) in the response. In essence, this method enables programmatic server-side includes. The ServletResponse object has its path elements and parameters remain unchanged from the caller's. The included servlet cannot change the response status code or set headers; any attempt to make a change is ignored.

Parameters:

request - a ServletRequest object that contains the client's request
response - a ServletResponse object that contains the servlet's response

Throws:

ServletException - if the included resource throws this exception
IOException - if the included resource throws this exception

getRequestDispatcher() method:
RequestDispatcher getRequestDispatcher(String path)
returns a RequestDispatcher object that acts as a wrapper for the resource located at the given path. A RequestDispatcher object can be used to forward a request to the resource or to include the resource in a response. The resource can be dynamic or static.

The pathname specified may be relative, although it cannot extend outside the current servlet context. If the path begins with a "/" it is interpreted as relative to the current context root. This method returns null if the servlet container cannot return a RequestDispatcher.

The difference between this method and Servlet Context.get Request Dispatcher(java.lang.String) is that this method can take a relative path.

SESSION AND THREAD MANAGEMENT

Session Management
Using session object:

The HttpSession API provides a simple mechanism for storing information about individual users on the application server. The API provides access to a session object that can be used to store other objects. The ability to tie objects to a particular user is important when working in an object-oriented environment.

It allows you to quickly and efficiently save and retrieve JavaBeans that you may be using to identify your site's visitors, to hold product information for display on your online store, or to track products that potential customers have placed in their shopping carts.

A session object is created on the application server, usually in a Java servlet or a JavaServerPage. The object is stored on the application server and a unique identifier called a session ID is assigned to it.

Advanced Web Tehnologies

The session object and session ID are handled by a session manager on the application server. Each session ID assigned by the application server has zero or more key/value pairs tied to it. The values are objects that you place in the session.

Assign each of those objects a name, and each name must have an object with it because a null is not allowed.

Using cookie:

A cookie is used to store the session ID on the Web site visitor's computer. This is automatically handled by the application server. Simply create the session object and begin using it.

The application server will, by default, create the session ID and store it in a cookie. The browser will send the cookie back to the server every time a page is requested. The application server, via the server's session manager, will match the session ID from the cookie to a session object.

The session object is then placed in the HttpServletRequest object and you retrieve it with the getSession() method.

Using URL rewritting:

The procedure for URL rewriting is quite simple and requires only the use of two methods found in the HttpServletResponse interface.

These two methods, encodeURL() and encodeRedirectURL(), are used to append the session ID to the URL. This allows the server to track users as they move through your Web pages, but it requires that every URL be rewritten.

The string returned by the methods will have the session ID appended to it only if the server determines that it's required. If the user's browser supports cookies, the returned URL will not be altered.

The following line of HTML code from a JSP creates a link to another JSP:

```
<A HREF="/products/product.jsp">Product Listing</A>
```

Clicking on this link would send the user to the product.jsp page.
Using URL rewriting, the same code would be written as follows:

```
<A HREF="
<%= response.encodeURL("/product/product.jsp")%>
">Product listing</A>
```

The returned string from the encodeURL() method would contain the session ID.
On a Tomcat 3.2 application server, the result of this line of code would be:

```
<A HREF="http://www.yourservername.com/products/ product.jsp;$sessionid$xxxx">
Product Listing
</A>
```

The xxxx would actually be a unique session ID generated by the server.

You should now have a good understanding of how the session ID is tracked and matched to a session object on the server.

The first step in using the session object is creating it. The method getSession() is used to create a new session object and to retrieve an already existing one. The getSession() method is passed a Boolean flag of true or false.

A false parameter indicates that you want to retrieve a session object that already exists. A true parameter lets the session manager know that a session object needs to be created if one does not already exist.

Following are some of the methods defined in the Java Servlet specification that can be used for session management:

setAttribute(String name, Object value): Binds an object to this session using the name specified. Returns nothing (void).

getAttribute(String name): Returns the object bound with the specified name in this session, or null if no object is bound under this name.

removeAttribute(String name): Removes the object bound with the specified name from this session. Returns nothing (void).

invalidate(): Invalidates this session and unbinds any objects bound to it. Returns nothing (void).

isNew(): Returns a Boolean with a value of true if the client does not yet know about the session or if the client chooses not to join the session.

EXAMPLE : you can save shopping cart as a session attribute.
This allows the shopping cart to be saved between requests and also allows cooperating servlets to access the cart. Some servlet adds items to the cart; another servlet displays, deletes items from, and clears the cart; and next servlet retrieves the total cost of the items in the cart.

```
public class CashierServlet extends HttpServlet
{
        public void doGet (HttpServletRequest req, HttpServletResponse
        res)throws ServletException, IOException
        {
                // Get the user's session and shopping cart HttpSession
                session = request.getSession();  ShoppingCart  cart  =
                (ShoppingCart) session.getAttribute("cart");
                ...
                // Determine the total price of the user's books double total
                = cart.getTotal();
                ...
        }
}
```

```
package javax.servlet.http;
public interface HttpSession
{
        public  java.lang.Object  getAttribute(java.lang.String  name);  public
        java.util.Enumeration getAttributeNames();
        public void removeAttribute(java.lang.String name);
        public void setAttribute(java.lang.String name, java.lang.Object value);

}
```

Thread Management

There are two major issues with Java Threads:

- Concurrency
- Control

Failure to address both these issues means the endeavor will fail sooner or later.

Java threads are most difficult to control. What if a thread gets stuck in a blocking method? What if something is wrong and the thread doesn't get CPU time? What if there is a bug? There are lots of 'what if'' situations.

Threads are not your traditional pool threads. Every Queue Thread has its own management structure. Each event in the life of a Queue Thread is timed.

Thread "interrupt()" is a disaster. The original developers probably had a vision that programmers would want to interrupt an executing thread. But they never perfected that vision. What we have now are threads interrupting themselves as well as other threads sometimes with erroneous results.

Let's say you create thread "A" and you expect that thread to complete some work within a time limit.
You execute a timed wait for thread "A".
Thread "A" does not complete within the time limit, the time expires and o you regain control.
Your code continues with other work.
Then you have a second timed wait for another thread "B".
If thread "A" then issues interrupt(), it interrupts the caller at the second wait.

Both NotifyAll() and SignalAll() are shot gun methods. Having multiple threads waiting on a single object is a course grained solution. When the group awakens every thread must do some work to find out if it is needed.

Even if each thread is running on a separate CPU it still requires operating system CPU cycles to get the threads running and put the unnecessary threads back into a blocking state.

The purpose of the wait(), notify() and notifyAll() methods is to temporarily pause and resume the execution of code in an object.

Typically the host object is not in a state where it can proceed with a method call it has been given and the thread of execution must literally wait for the object to return to a ready state. A common example would be a limited pool or store of objects where you must wait for a storage slot to be released or an object to be returned to the pool before you can use it.

```
public synchronized Object getNextObject() {
// Waiting loop
while (! objectAvailable())
{
try {
        wait();
}
catch (InterruptedException e)
        {
Handle exception
}
}
```

No longer waiting, get the return object Object returnObject;
    Assign the returnObject from store
    Notify state change for other waiters notify();

            return returnObject;
    }

The act of waiting is associated with the Object class because any subclass may need to wait for a ready state to occur.
The waiting process acts on a single thread of execution, but the wait mechanism expects that multiple threads may be waiting for the same object. The wait and notify methods are hosted by the Object class so that the Java Virtual

Exercise:
        What is JSP?
        Why JSP is required? Also explain when it is required?
        Explain the architectural model of JSP?
        Explain the different components of JSP?
        Explain the expression used in JSP programs?
        What is scriplet?
        What is difference between HTML tag and scriplet tag?
        Write a note on Thread Management?

4

INTRODUCTION TO WEB SERVICES

WHAT IS A WEB SERVICE?

Definition:

A Web service is a software system designed to support interoperable machine-to-machine interaction over a network. It has an interface described in a machine-processable format
(specifically WSDL). Other systems interact with the Web service in a manner prescribed by its description using SOAP messages, typically conveyed using HTTP with an XML serialization in conjunction with other Web-related standards.

Agents and Services

A Web service is an abstract notion that must be implemented by a concrete agent. The agent is the concrete piece of software or hardware that sends and receives messages, while the service is the resource characterized by the abstract set of functionality that is provided. To illustrate this distinction, you might implement a particular Web service using one agent one day (perhaps written in one programming language), and a different agent the next day (perhaps written in a different programming language) with the same functionality. Although the agent may have changed, the Web service remains the same.

Requesters and Providers

The purpose of a Web service is to provide some functionality on behalf of its owner -- a person or organization, such as a business or an individual. The *provider entity* is the person or organization that provides an appropriate agent to implement a particular service. A *requester entity* is a person or organization that wishes to make use of a provider entity's Web service. It will use a *requester agent* to exchange messages with the provider entity's *provider agent*.

(In most cases, the requester agent is the one to initiate this message exchange, though not always. Nonetheless, for consistency we still use the term "requester agent" for the agent that interacts with the provider agent, even in cases when the provider agent actually initiates the exchange.)

Note:
A word on terminology: Many documents use the term service provider to refer to the provider entity and/or provider agent. Similarly, they may use the term service requester to refer to the requester entity and/or requester agent. However, since these terms are ambiguous -- sometimes referring to the agent and sometimes to the person or organization that owns the agent -- this document prefers the terms *requester entity*, *provider entity*, *requester agent* and *provider agent*.

In order for this message exchange to be successful, the requester entity and the provider entity must first agree on both the semantics and the mechanics of the message exchange.

Service Description

The mechanics of the message exchange are documented in a Web service description (WSD). The WSD is a machine-processable specification of the Web service's interface, written in WSDL. It defines the message formats, datatypes, transport protocols, and transport serialization formats that should be used between the requester agent and the provider agent. It also specifies one or more network locations at which a provider agent can be invoked, and may provide some information about the message exchange pattern that is expected. In essence, the service description represents an agreement governing the mechanics of interacting with that service.

Semantics

The semantics of a Web service is the shared expectation about the behavior of the service, in particular in response to messages that are sent to it. In effect, this is the "contract" between the requester entity and the provider entity regarding the purpose and consequences of the interaction. Although this contract represents the overall agreement between the requester entity and the provider entity on how and why their respective agents will interact, it is not necessarily written or explicitly negotiated. It may be explicit or implicit, oral or written, machine processable or human oriented, and it may be a legal agreement or an informal (non-legal) agreement.

While the service description represents a contract governing the mechanics of interacting with a particular service, the semantics represents a contract governing the meaning and purpose of that interaction. The dividing line between these two is not necessarily rigid. As more semantically rich languages are used to describe the mechanics of the interaction, more of the essential information may migrate from the informal semantics to the service description. As this migration occurs, more of the work required to achieve successful interaction can be automated.

Advanced Web Tehnologies

Overview of Engaging a Web Service

There are many ways that a requester entity might engage and use a Web service. In general, the following broad steps are required:

- The requester and provider entities become known to each other (or at least one becomes know to the other);

- The requester and provider entities somehow agree on the service description and semantics that will govern the interaction between the requester and provider agents;
- The service description and semantics are realized by the requester and provider agents;
- The requester and provider agents exchange messages, thus performing some task on behalf of the requester and provider entities. (I.e., the exchange of messages with the provider agent represents the concrete manifestation of interacting with the provider entity's Web service.)

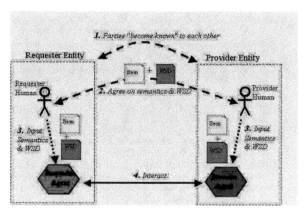

The General Process of Engaging a Web Service

SOFTWARE AS A SERVICE

Definition:

Software as a Service (SaaS) is a software distribution model in which applications are hosted by a vendor or service provider and made available to customers over a network, typically the Internet.

SaaS is becoming an increasingly prevalent delivery model as underlying technologies that support Web services and service-oriented architecture (SOA) mature and new developmental approaches, such as Ajax, become popular.

Meanwhile, broadband service has become increasingly available to support user access from more areas around the world.

VSaaS is closely related to the ASP (application service provider) and On Demand Computing software delivery models.
IDC identifies two slightly different delivery models for SaaS. The hosted application management (hosted AM) model is similar to ASP: a provider hosts commercially available software for customers and delivers it over the Web. In the software on demand model, the provider gives customers network-based access to a single copy of an application created specifically for SaaS distribution.

Key characteristics

SaaS characteristics include:

Network-based access to, and management of, commercially available software
Activities managed from central locations rather than at each customer's site, enabling customers to access applications remotely via the Web
Application delivery typically closer to a one-to-many model (single instance, multi-tenant architecture) than to a one-to-one model, including architecture, pricing, partnering, and management characteristics
Centralized feature updating, which obviates the need for end-users to download patches and upgrades.
Frequent integration into a larger network of communicating software—either as part of a mashup or a plugin to a platform as a service (Service oriented architecture is naturally more complex than traditional models of software deployment.)

SaaS providers generally price applications on a per-user basis and/or per business basis, sometimes with a relatively small minimum number of users and often with additional fees for extra bandwidth and storage. SaaS revenue streams to the vendor are therefore lower initially than traditional software license fees, but are also recurring, and therefore viewed as more predictable, much like maintenance fees for licensed software.
In addition to characteristics mentioned above, SaaS sometimes provides:

More feature requests from users, since there is frequently no marginal cost for requesting new features

Faster new feature releases, since the entire community of users benefits

Embodiment of recognized best practices, since the user community drives the software publisher to support best practice

Benefits

Benefits of the SaaS model include:

- easier administration
- automatic updates and patch management
- compatibility: All users will have the same version of software.
- easier collaboration, for the same reason
- global accessibility.

The traditional model of software distribution, in which software is purchased for and installed on personal computers, is sometimes referred to as *software as a product.*

WEB SERVICE ARCHITECTURES

Purpose of the Web Service Architecture

Web services provide a standard means of interoperating between different software applications, running on a variety of platforms and/or frameworks. This document (WSA) is intended to provide a common definition of a Web service, and define its place within a larger Web services framework to guide the community. The WSA provides a conceptual model and a context for understanding Web services and the relationships between the components of this model. The architecture does not attempt to specify how Web services are implemented, and imposes no restriction on how Web services might be combined. The WSA describes both the minimal characteristics that are common to all Web services, and a number of characteristics that are needed by many, but not all, Web services. The Web services architecture is interoperability architecture: it identifies those global elements of the global Web services network that are required in order to ensure interoperability between Web services.

There are two ways to view the web service architecture.

- The first is to examine the individual roles of each web service actor.
- The second is to examine the emerging web service protocol stack.

1. Web Service Roles

There are three major roles within the web service architecture:

Service provider:
This is the provider of the web service. The service provider implements the service and makes it available on the Internet.

Service requestor
This is any consumer of the web service. The requestor utilizes an existing web service by opening a network connection and sending an XML request.

Service registry
This is a logically centralized directory of services. The registry provides a central place where developers can publish new services or find existing ones. It therefore serves as a centralized clearinghouse for companies and their services.

2. Web Service Protocol Stack
A second option for viewing the web service architecture is to examine the emerging web service protocol stack. The stack is still evolving, but currently has four main layers.

Service transport
This layer is responsible for transporting messages between applications. Currently, this layer includes hypertext transfer protocol (HTTP), Simple Mail Transfer Protocol (SMTP), file transfer protocol (FTP), and newer protocols, such as Blocks Extensible Exchange Protocol (BEEP).

XML messaging
This layer is responsible for encoding messages in a common XML format so that messages can be understood at either end. Currently, this layer includes XML-RPC and SOAP.

Service description
This layer is responsible for describing the public interface to a specific web service. Currently, service description is handled via the Web Service Description Language (WSDL).

Service discovery
This layer is responsible for centralizing services into a common registry, and providing easy publish/find functionality.
Currently, service discovery is handled via Universal Description, Discovery, and Integration (UDDI).

As web services evolve, additional layers may be added, and additional technologies may be added to each layer.

Advanced Web Tehnologies

Few Words about Service Transport

The bottom of the web service protocol stack is service transport. This layer is responsible for actually transporting XML messages between two computers.

Hyper Text Transfer Protocol (HTTP)

Currently, HTTP is the most popular option for service transport. HTTP is simple, stable, and widely deployed.
Furthermore, most firewalls allow HTTP traffic. This allows XMLRPC or SOAP messages to masquerade as HTTP messages.
This is good if you want to easily integrate remote applications, but it does raise a number of security concerns.

Blocks Extensible Exchange Protocol (BEPP)

One promising alternative to HTTP is the Blocks Extensible Exchange Protocol (BEEP).BEEP is a new IETF framework of best practices for building new protocols. BEEP is layered directly on TCP and includes a number of built-in features, including an initial handshake protocol, authentication, security, and error handling.
Using BEEP, one can create new protocols for a variety of applications, including instant messaging, file transfer, content syndication, and network management

SOAP is not tied to any specific transport protocol. In fact, you can use SOAP via HTTP, SMTP, or FTP. One promising idea is therefore to use SOAP over BEEP.

SOA (Service Oriented Architecture)

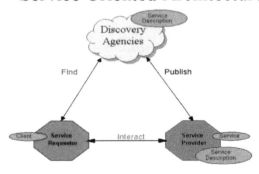

Advanced Web Tehnologies

The figure above illustrates the relationships between requesters, providers, services, descriptions, and discovery services in the case where agents take on both requester and provider roles. For example, XML messages compliant with the SOAP specification are exchanged between the requester and provider. The provider publishes a WSDL file that contains a description of the message and endpoint information to allow the requester to generate the SOAP message and send it to the correct destination.

To support the common MEP of request/response, for example, a Web services implementation provides software agents that function as both requesters and providers, as shown in Figure.
The service requester sends a message in the form of a request for information, or to perform an operation, and receives a message from the service provider that contains the result of the request or operation. The service provider receives the request, processed the message and sends a response. The technologies typically used for this type of Web services interaction include SOAP, WSDL, and HTTP.

Note:
The Web services architecture does not include the concept of automatically correlating requests and responses, as some RPC oriented technologies do. The correletion of request and response messages is typically application-defined.

The following sections provide more formal definitions of the components, roles, and operations in Web services architecture.

Components

The Service: Whereas a web service is an interface described by a service description, its implementation is the service. A service is a software module deployed on network accessible platforms provided by the service provider. It exists to be invoked by or to interact with a service requestor. It may also function as a requestor, using other web services in its implementation.

The Service Description: The service description contains the details of the interface and implementation of the service. This includes its data types, operations, binding information, and network location. It could also include categorization and other meta data to facilitate discovery and utilization by requestors.
The complete description may be realized as a set of XML description documents. The service description may be published to a requestor directly or to a discovery agency.

Roles

Service Provider: From a business perspective, this is the owner of the service. From an architectural perspective, this is the platform that hosts access to the service. It has also been referred to as a service execution environment or a service container. Its role in the client-server message exchange patterns is that of a server.

Service Requestor: From a business perspective, this is the business that requires certain function to be satisfied. From an architectural perspective, this is the application that is looking for and invoking or initiating an interaction with a service. The requestor role can be played by a browser driven by a person or a program without a user interface, e.g. another web service. Its role in the client-server message exchange patters is that of a client.

Discovery Agency: This is a searchable set of service descriptions where service providers publish their service descriptions. The service discovery agency can be centralized or distributed. A discovery agency can support both the pattern where it has descriptions sent to it and where the agency actively inspects public providers for descriptions. Service requestors may find services and obtain binding information (in the service descriptions) during development for static binding, or during execution for dynamic binding. For statically bound service requestors, the service discovery agent is in fact an optional role in the architecture, as a service provider can send the description directly to service requestors. Likewise, service requestors can obtain a service description from other sources besides a service registry, such as a local filesystem, FTP site, URL, or WSIL document.

Operations

In order for an application to take advantage of Web services, three behaviors must take place: publication of service descriptions, finding and retrieval of service descriptions, and binding or invoking of services based on the service description.

These behaviors can occur singly or iteratively, with any cardinality between the roles. In detail these operations are:

Publish: In order to be accessible, a service needs to publish its description such that the requestor can subsequently find it.
Where it is published can vary depending upon the requirements of the application (see Service Publication Stack discussion for more details)

Find: In the find operation, the service requestor retrieves a service description directly or queries the registry for the type of service required (see Service Discovery for more details). The find operation may be involved in two different lifecycle phases for the service requestor: at design time in order to retrieve the service's interface description for program development, and at runtime in order to retrieve the service's binding and location description for invocation.

Interact: Eventually, a service needs to be invoked. In the interact operation the service requestor invokes or initiates an interaction with the service at runtime using the binding details in the service description to locate, contact, and invoke the service. Examples of the interaction include: single message one way, broadcast from requester to many services, a multi message conversation, or a business process. Any of these types of interactions can be synchronous or asynchronous.

XML

What is XML?

XML (Extensible Markup Language) is a set of rules for encoding documents in machine-readable form. It is defined in the XML 1.0 Specification[4] produced by the W3C, and several other related specifications, all gratis open standards.[5]

XML's design goals emphasize simplicity, generality, and usability over the Internet.[6] It is a textual data format, with strong support via Unicode for the languages of the world. Although XML's design focuses on documents, it is widely used for the representation of arbitrary data structures, for example in web services.

There are many programming interfaces that software developers may use to access XML data, and several schema systems designed to aid in the definition of XML-based languages.

As of 2009, hundreds of XML-based languages have been developed, including RSS, Atom, SOAP, and XHTML. XML-based formats have become the default for most office-productivity tools, including Microsoft Office (Office Open XML), OpenOffice.org (OpenDocument), and Apple's iWork.

Exercise:
What is Web service?
Explain the concept of SOA?
State and explain the characteristics of Software as service?
Explain the role of service providers in SOA model?
Explain the XML technology in detail?
Explain the architectural view of web services?

5

INTRODUCTION TO .NET FRAMEWORK

The .NET History

Sometime in the July 2000, Microsoft announced a whole new software development framework for Windows called .NET in the Professional Developer Conference (PDC). Microsoft also released PDC version of the software for the developers to test. After initial testing and feedback Beta 1 of .NET was announced. Beta 1 of the .NET itself got lot of attention from the developer community. When Microsoft announced Beta 2, it incorporated many changes suggested by the community and internals into the software. The overall 'Beta' phase lasted for more than 1 ½ years. Finally, in March 2002 Microsoft released final version of the .NET framework.

> One thing to be noted here is the change in approach of Microsoft while releasing this new platform. Unlike other software where generally only a handful people are involved in beta testing,

.NET was thrown open to community for testing in it's every pre-release version. This is one of the reasons why it created so many waves of excitement within the community and industry as well.

Microsoft has put in great efforts in this new platform. In fact Microsoft says that its future depends on success of .NET. The development of .NET is such an important event that Microsoft considers it equivalent to transition from DOS to Windows. All the future development – including new and version upgrades of existing products – will revolve around .NET.

Flavors of .NET

Contrary to general belief .NET is not a single technology. Rather it is a set of technologies that work together seamlessly to solve your business problems. The following sections will give you insight into various flavors and tools of .NET and what kind of applications you can develop.

What type of applications can I develop?

When you hear the name .NET, it gives a feeling that it is something to do only with internet or networked applications. Even though it is true that .NET provides solid foundation for developing such applications it is possible to create many other types of applications. Following list will give you an idea about various types of application that we can develop on .NET.

ASP.NET Web applications: These include dynamic and data driven browser based applications.

Windows Form based applications: These refer to traditional rich client applications.

Console applications: These refer to traditional DOS kind of applications like batch scripts.

Component Libraries: This refers to components that typically encapsulate some business logic.

Windows Custom Controls: As with traditional ActiveX controls, you can develop your own windows controls.

Web Custom Controls: The concept of custom controls can be extended to web applications allowing code reuse and modularization.

Web services: They are "web callable" functionality available via industry standards like HTTP, XML and SOAP.

Windows Services: They refer to applications that run as services in the background. They can be configured to start automatically when the system boots up.

As you can clearly see, .NET is not just for creating web application but for almost all kinds of applications that you find under Windows.

.NET Framework SDK

You can develop such varied types of applications. That's fine. But how? As with most of the programming languages, .NET .has a complete Software Development Kit (SDK) – more commonly referred to as .NET Framework SDK – that provides classes, interfaces and language compilers necessary to program for .NET.

Additionally it contains excellent documentation and Quick Start tutorials that help you learn .NET technologies with ease. Good news is that - .NET Framework SDK is available FREE of cost. You can download it from the MSDN web site. This means that if you have machine with .NET Framework installed and a text editor such as Notepad then you can start developing for .NET right now!

You can download entire .NET Framework SDK (approx 131 Mb) from MSDN web site at http://msdn.microsoft.com/downloads/default.asp?url=/downloads/sample.asp?url=/msdn-files/027/000/976/msdncompositedoc.xml

Development Tools

If you are developing applications that require speedy delivery to your customers and features like integration with some version control software then simple Notepad may not serve your purpose. In such cases you require some Integrated Development Environment (IDE) that allows for Rapid Action Development (RAD). The new Visual Studio.NET is such an IDE. VS.NET is a powerful and flexible IDE that makes developing .NET applications a breeze. Some of the features of VS.NET that make you more productive are:

- Drag and Drop design
- IntelliSense features
- Syntax highlighting and auto-syntax checking
- Excellent debugging tools
- Integration with version control software such as Visual Source Safe (VSS)
- Easy project management

Note that when you install Visual Studio.NET, .NET Framework is automatically installed on the machine.

Visual Studio.NET Editions

Visual Studio.NET comes in different editions. You can select edition appropriate for the kind of development you are doing. Following editions of VS.NET are available:

- Professional
- Enterprise Developer
- Enterprise Architect

Visual Studio .NET Professional edition offers a development tool for creating various types of applications mentioned previously. Developers can use Professional edition to build Internet and Develop applications quickly and create solutions that span any device and integrate with any platform.

Visual Studio .NET Enterprise Developer (VSED) edition contains all the features of Professional edition plus has additional capabilities for enterprise development. The features include things such as a collaborative team development, Third party tool integration for building XML Web services and built -in project templates with architectural guidelines and spanning comprehensive project life-cycle.

Visual Studio .NET Enterprise Architect (VSEA) edition contains all the features of Visual Studio .NET Enterprise Developer edition and additionally includes capabilities for designing, specifying, and communicating application architecture and functionality. The additional features include Visual designer for XML Web services, Unified Modeling Language (UML) support and enterprise templates for development guidelines and policies.

Special language specific editions are available. They are:
- Visual Basic.NET Standard Edition
- Visual C# Standard Edition
- Visual C++ .NET Standard (soon to be released)

Introduction to .NET Framework

The Microsoft .NET Framework is a software framework that can be installed on computers running Microsoft Windows operating systems. It includes a large library of coded solutions to common programming problems and a virtual machine that manages the execution of programs written specifically for the framework. The .NET Framework supports multiple programming languages in a manner that allows language interoperability, whereby each language can utilize code written in other languages; in particular, the .NET library is available to all the programming languages that .NET encompasses. The .NET Framework is a Microsoft offering and is intended to be used by most new applications created for the Windows platform. In order to be able to develop and not just run applications for the Microsoft .NET Framework 4.0, it is required to have Visual Studio 2010 installed on your computer.

The framework's Base Class Library provides a large range of features including user interface, data access, database connectivity, cryptography, web application development, numeric algorithms, and network communications. The class library is used by programmers, who combine it with their own code to produce applications.

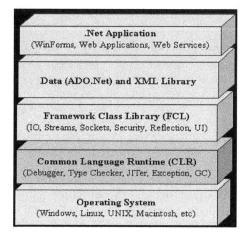

Microsoft .NET Framework

EVOLUTION OF .NET

The Microsoft .NET initiative is all-encompassing, ever-present, and in certain ways, brand-new—but the underlying technologies have been with us for some time. In this article, we'll explore the evolutionary process that made .NET possible, from MS-DOS and the iterations of Windows to ActiveX. It's all come together to culminate in .NET C:\DOS\Run (MS-DOS)

DOS carved its spot in computing history as the innovation that let regular folks use computers. Prior to that, no *one* user ever operated a computer. It was always operated by a *team* of users.

When DOS came out in 1981, a couple of companies (most notably, Novell) built software to let teams work on bundles of computers—the first PC-based networks. Other companies built products like Telix, PCBoard and Wildcat, enabling the building of the first distributed public networks. The DOS world was great, but everything changed when Microsoft invented Windows. C:\Windows\Run (Win3.1)

Next came Windows, a GUI even your grandmother could use. The old standby, MS-DOS, was still with us working in the background behind Windows. The first widely accepted iteration of this revolutionary product was Windows 3.1; networking was introduced with 3.11. Users could share files and folders graphically and even send e-mail without having to use the cryptic command-line tool.

With Windows making the PC easier to use, suddenly it became simple to access huge, legacy databases. All this easy access began to tax the resources of mainframes. More efficient use of valuable network resources was needed.

C:\Windows\Crash (Win32)

Microsoft learned early that regular and recurring releases raise revenue. No product can be everything to every user, and bugs needed to be fixed, so constant upgrades and new product releases were necessary. With each release, new features (and bugs) were introduced.

The first release of Win32 was Windows 95. This was a big change, moving from a 16-bit system in Windows 3.x and MS-
DOS to a 32-bit operating system in Windows 95. This new version contained robust networking features and tools out of the box. This included standard TCP/IP support and wizards to automate network access/setup.

About the same time, and between Microsoft's planned releases, the World Wide Web blew onto the scene. To effectively support the networking features required to connect users to their
ISPs, Microsoft released a couple of service releases and, finally, Windows 98.

Activate the Internet (ActiveX)

When Bill Gates takes one of his famous reading vacations, the result usually affects the course of information technology for years to come. Gates had made a fortune producing operating systems and software for the PC; now he realized another fortune could be made in producing software for the Internet. Upon returning from a mid-1990s reading vacation, he handed down a decree to Microsoft employees: Activate the Internet. Thus, ActiveX technologies were born.
ActiveX is a reworking of Microsoft's component format, the OLE/COM technology found in all Microsoft products. ActiveX, which emerged as the cornerstone of Microsoft's plans (at the time), encompassed all of the current Internet technologies in "objects." Object-oriented programming was all the rage, requiring different components to work well with and within each other.
ActiveX would extend that model to include the object's context (such as a desktop application or a Web script) or the environment in which it would run (e.g., over a slow network).

For a time, it looked like Microsoft was going to make the Sun Java technologies a subset of ActiveX. Such a partnership would undoubtedly have benefited both. A few dozen lawsuits and an antitrust case later, however, the split is complete.

Dot Net (.NET)

The advent of .NET brings us to the present. The .NET initiative continues the evolution of the Microsoft technologies including ActiveX and the doomed DNA product. Its extensive support for open standards constitutes an apparent paradigm shift for Microsoft.

Microsoft software has the lion's share of almost every software market out there, but the market is changing fast. The key to remember here is that .NET is a *server* technology initiative. It doesn't matter what client software you're using; it doesn't even matter if you're running a cell phone, PDA, wristwatch, or toaster instead of a PC. The client market has become a commodity system. The important stuff is on the server... or servers.

Advanced Web Tehnologies

Building an application that tracks an individual or organization's personal, professional, and other information is easy. Any MCSD, MCDBA, Perl, or Java guru can do it in a flash and for a song. Building a suite of applications, with different physical and conceptual architectures, availability requirements, and resources, is a whole other ballgame. The adoption of both existing and emerging open standards like XML promises to ease the burden of integrating disparate systems. This is one of the goals of the .NET framework.

COMPARISON OF JAVA AND .NET

At root level architecture and components, MS.NET and J2EE platforms are very similar. Both are virtual machine based architecture having CLR and Java Virtual Machine (JVM) as the underlying virtual machine for the management and execution of programs. Both provide memory, security and thread management on behalf of the program and both try to decouple the applications with the execution environment (OS and physical machine). Both, basically, target the Web based applications and especially the XML based web services. Both provide managed access to memory and no direct access to memory is allowed to their managed applications.

However, there are few contrasts in the architecture and design of the two virtual machines. Microsoft .NET framework's architecture is more coupled to the Microsoft Windows Operating System which makes it difficult to implement it on various operating systems and physical machines. Java, on the other hand, is available on almost all major platforms. At the darker side, J2EE architecture and JVM is more coupled to the Java programming language while Microsoft.NET has been designed from the scratch to support language independence and language integration. Microsoft.NET covers the component development and integration in much more detail than Java. The versioning policy of .NET is simply the best implemented versioning solution in the software development history. Java has got the support of industry giants like Sun, IBM, Apache and Oracle while the Microsoft.NET is supported by giants like Microsoft, Intel, and HP.

Advanced Web Tehnologies

ARCHITECTURE OF .NET FRAMEWORK

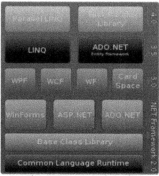

The .NET Framework Stack

Common Language Runtime

The Common Language Runtime (CLR) is a core component of Microsoft's .NET initiative. It is Microsoft's implementation of the Common Language Infrastructure (CLI) standard, which defines an execution environment for program code. In the CLR, code is expressed in a form of bytecode called the Common Intermediate Language (CIL, previously known as MSIL—Microsoft Intermediate Language).

Developers using the CLR write code in a language such as C# or VB.NET. At compile time, a .NET compiler converts such code into CIL code. At runtime, the CLR's just-in-time compiler converts the CIL code into code native to the operating system. Alternatively, the CIL code can be compiled to native code in a separate step prior to runtime by using the Native Image Generator (NGEN). This speeds up all later runs of the software as the CIL-to-native compilation is no longer necessary.

Although some other implementations of the Common Language Infrastructure run on non-Windows operating systems, Microsoft's implementation runs only on Microsoft Windows operating systems

Common Type System

Advanced Web Tehnologies

CTS - Common Type System

The Common Type System, support both Object Oriented Programming like Java as well as Procedural languages like 'C'. It deals with two kinds of entities: Objects and Values. Values are the familiar atomic types like integers and chars. Objects are self defining entities containing both methods and variables.

Objects and Values can be categorized into the following hierarchy:

Types can be of two kinds Value Types and Reference Types. Value Types can further categorized into built-in (for example Integer Types and Float Type) and user defined types like Enum.

Reference Type can be divided into three sub categories: Self Describing Reference Type, Pointers and Interfaces. Pointers can be sub divided into Function pointers, Managed and Unmanaged Types.

Value Types can be converted into Reference Type, and this conversion is called Boxing of Values. De-referencing the Boxed
Value Types from the Referenced Type is called Un-Boxing.

Casting rules from one type to another, for example conversion of char to integer types are also defined within the Common Type System.

Common Type System also defines scope and assemblies. An assembly is a configured set of loadable code modules and other resources that together implement a unit of functionality. A scope is a collection of grouped names of different kinds of values or reference types.

Metadata

.NET metadata, in the Microsoft .NET framework, refers to certain data structures embedded within the Common Intermediate
Language code that describes the high-level structure of the code.
Metadata describes all classes and class members that are defined in the assembly, and the classes and class members that the current assembly will call from another assembly. The metadata for a method contains the complete description of the method, including the class (and the assembly that contains the class), the return type and all of the method parameters.

A .NET language compiler will generate the metadata and store this in the assembly containing the CIL. When the CLR executes CIL it will check to make sure that the metadata of the called method is the same as the metadata that is stored in the calling method. This ensures that a method can only be called with exactly the right number of parameters and exactly the right parameter types

Assemblies

An assembly is the functional unit of sharing and reuse in the Common Language Runtime. It is the equivalent of JAR (Java Archive) files of Java.

Assembly is a collection of physical files package in a .CAB format or newly introduced .MSI file format. The assemblies contained in a .CAB or .MSI files are called static assemblies, they include .NET Framework types (interfaces and classes) as well as resources for the assembly (bitmaps, JPEG files, resource files, etc.). They also include metadata that eliminates the need of IDL file descriptors, which were required for describing COM components.

The Common Language Runtime also provide API's that script engines use to create dynamic assemblies when executing scripts. These assemblies are run directly and are never saved to disk.

Microsoft has greatly diminished the role of Windows
Registry system with introduction of assemblies concept, which is an adaptation of Java's JAR deployment technology.

Assemblies is an adaptation, but not a copy of Java's JAR technology. It has been improved upon in some ways, for example it has introduced a versioning system. However, since the .NET framework is skewed towards the Windows architecture some of the Java's JAR portability features may have been sacrificed.

Again, similar to JAR files, the assemblies too contain an entity called manifest. However, manifest in .NET framework plays somewhat wider role. Manifest is a metadata describing the inter-relationship between the entities contained in the assemblies like managed code, images and multimedia resources. Manifest also specifies versioning information.

> The manifest is basically a deployment descriptor, having XML syntax. Java programmers can relate it with J2EE (Java 2 Enterprise Edition) deployment descriptors for EjB (Enterprise Java Beans) applications.

The Microsoft documentation stress that assemblies are "logical dlls". This may be a reasonable paradigm for VB or C++ programmers, but Java programmers will find it easier, if we visualize assemblies as an extension of JAR concept. However, unlike JAR, each assembly can have only one entry point defined, which can be either DllMain, WinMain, or Main.

As stated earlier, Assemblies have a manifest metadata. This contains version and digitally signed information. This purports to implement version control and authentication of the software developer. Version and authentication procedure is carried out by the runtime during loading the assembly into the code execution area.

Again, much like Java's trusted lib. concept, .NET Assemblies can be placed in secured area called global assembly cache. This area is equivalent to trusted class path of Java. Only system administrators can install or deinstall Assemblies from the global assembly cache. There is a place for downloaded or transient Assemblies called downloaded assembly cache. The Assemblies loaded from global assembly cache run outside the sandbox and have faster load time as well as enjoy more freedom to access file system resources. The Assemblies loaded from the downloaded cache area are subject to more security checks, therefore are slower to load and since they run inside the sandbox; enjoy much less privileges.

Assemblies manifests also contain information regarding sharing of code by different Applications and Application Domains.

To summarize, the Operating System can have multiple applications running simultaneously, each such application occupies a separate Win32 process and can contain multiple
Application Domains. An Application Domain can be constructed from multiple assemblies.

Application Domains

Application domains are light weight process. It can be visualized as an extension of Java's sandbox security and Thread model.

The Common Language Runtime provides a secure, lightweight unit of processing called an application domain.
Application domains also enforce security policy.

By light weight it means that multiple application domains run in a single Win32 process, yet they provide a kind of fault isolation, that is fault in one application domain does not corrupt other application domains. This aids in enhancing execution security against viruses as well as helps in debugging faulty codes.

The Common Language Runtime relies on type safety and verifiability features of Common Type System (CTS) to provide fault isolation between application domains. Since type verification can be conducted statically before execution, it is cost efficient and needs less security support from microprocessor hardware.

Each application can have multiple application domains associated with it. And each application domain has a configuration file, containing security permissions. This configuration information is used by the Common Language Runtime to provide sandbox security similar to that of Java sandbox model.

Although multiple application domains can run within a process, no direct calls are allowed between methods of objects in different application domains. Instead, a proxy mechanism is used for code space isolation.

Advanced Web Tehnologies

FCL (Framework class library)

.NET Framework provides huge set of Framework (or Base) Class Library (FCL) for common, usual tasks. FCL contains thousands of classes to provide the access to Windows API and common functions like String Manipulation, Common Data Structures, IO, Streams, Threads, Security, Network Programming, Windows Programming, Web Programming, Data Access, etc. It is simply the largest standard library ever shipped with any development environment or programming language. The best part of this library is they follow extremely efficient OO design (design patterns) making their access and use very simple and predictable.

You can use the classes in FCL in your program just as you use any other class and can even apply inheritance and polymorphism on these.

FEATURES OF .NET

Interoperability

Because interaction between new and older applications is commonly required, the .NET Framework provides means to access functionality that is implemented in programs that execute outside the .NET environment. Access to COM components is provided in the System. Runtime.Interop Services and System.EnterpriseServices namespaces of the framework; access to other functionality is provided using the P/Invoke feature.

Common Runtime Engine

The Common Language Runtime (CLR) is the virtual machine component of the .NET Framework. All .NET programs execute under the supervision of the CLR, guaranteeing certain properties and behaviors in the areas of memory management, security, and exception handling.

Language Independence

The .NET Framework introduces a Common Type System, or CTS. The CTS specification defines all possible datatypes and programming constructs supported by the CLR and how they may or may not interact with each other conforming to the Common Language Infrastructure (CLI) specification. Because of this feature, the .NET Framework supports the exchange of types and object instances between libraries and applications written using any conforming .NET language.

Base Class Library

The Base Class Library (BCL), part of the Framework Class Library (FCL), is a library of functionality available to all languages using the .NET Framework. The

BCL provides classes which encapsulate a number of common functions, including file reading and writing, graphic rendering, database interaction, XML document manipulation and so on.

Simplified Deployment

The .NET Framework includes design features and tools that help manage the installation of computer software to ensure that it does not interfere with previously installed software, and that it conforms to security requirements.

Security

The design is meant to address some of the vulnerabilities, such as buffer overflows, that have been exploited by malicious software. Additionally, .NET provides a common security model for all applications.

Portability

The design of the .NET Framework allows it to theoretically be platform agnostic, and thus cross-platform compatible. That is, a program written to use the framework should run without change on any type of system for which the framework is implemented. While Microsoft has never implemented the full framework on any system except Microsoft Windows, the framework is engineered to be platform agnostic, and cross-platform implementations are available for other operating systems (see Silverlight and the Alternative implementations section below). Microsoft submitted the specifications for the Common Language Infrastructure (which includes the core class libraries, Common Type System, and the Common Intermediate Language), the C# language, and the C++/CLI language to both ECMA and the ISO, making them available as open standards. This makes it possible for third parties to create compatible implementations of the framework and its languages on other platforms.

ADVANTAGES AND APPLICATION

Advantages:

Consistent Programming Model

Different programming languages have different approaches for doing a task. For example, accessing data with a VB 6.0 application and a VC++ application is totally different. When using different programming languages to do a task, a disparity exists among the approach developers use to perform the task. The difference in techniques comes from how different languages interact with the underlying system that applications rely on.

With .NET, for example, accessing data with a VB .NET and a C# .NET looks very similar apart from slight syntactical differences. Both the programs need to import the System.Data namespace, both the programs establish a connection with the database and both the programs run a query and display the data on a data grid. The VB 6.0 and VC++ example mentioned in the first paragraph explains that there is more than one way to do a particular task within the same language. The .NET example explains that there's a unified means of accomplishing the same task by using the .NET Class Library, a key component of the .NET Framework.

The functionality that the .NET Class Library provides is available to all .NET languages resulting in a consistent object model regardless of the programming language the developer uses.

Direct Support for Security

Developing an application that resides on a local machine and uses local resources is easy. In this scenario, security isn't an issue as all the resources are available and accessed locally.
Consider an application that accesses data on a remote machine or has to perform a privileged task on behalf of a nonprivileged user. In this scenario security is much more important as the application is accessing data from a remote machine.

With .NET, the Framework enables the developer and the system administrator to specify method level security. It uses industry-standard protocols such as TCP/IP, XML, SOAP and HTTP to facilitate distributed application communications. This makes distributed computing more secure because .NET developers cooperate with network security devices instead of working around their security limitations.

Simplified Development Efforts

Let's take a look at this with Web applications. With classic ASP, when a developer needs to present data from a database in a Web page, he is required to write the application logic (code) and presentation logic (design) in the same file. He was required to mix the ASP code with the HTML code to get the desired result.

ASP.NET and the .NET Framework simplify development by separating the application logic and presentation logic making it easier to maintain the code. You write the design code (presentation logic) and the actual code (application logic) separately eliminating the need to mix HTML code with ASP code. ASP.NET can also handle the details of maintaining the state of the controls, such as contents in a textbox, between calls to the same ASP.NET page.

Another advantage of creating applications is debugging. Visual Studio .NET and other third party providers provide several debugging tools that simplify application development. The .NET Framework simplifies debugging with support for Runtime diagnostics. Runtime diagnostics helps you to track down bugs and also helps you to determine how well an application performs. The .NET Framework provides three types of Runtime diagnostics: Event Logging, Performance Counters and Tracing.

Easy Application Deployment and Maintenance

The .NET Framework makes it easy to deploy applications. In the most common form, to install an application, all you need to do is copy the application along with the components it requires into a directory on the target computer. The .NET Framework handles the details of locating and loading the components an application needs, even if several versions of the same application exist on the target computer. The .NET Framework ensures that all the components the application depends on are available on the computer before the application begins to execute.

Real World Application

Microsoft's passport service is an example of a .NET service. Passport is a Web-based service designed to make signing in to Websites fast and easy. Passport enables participating sites to authenticate a user with a single set of sign-in credentials eliminating the need for users to remember numerous passwords and sign-in names. You can use one name and password to sign in to all .NET Passport-participating sites and services. You can store personal information in your .NET Passport profile and, if you choose, automatically share that information when you sign in so that participating sites can provide you with personalized services. If you use Hotmail for your email needs then you should be very much familiar with the passport service.

To find out more about how Businesses are implementing Web Services and the advantages it is providing please visit Microsoft's Website and check out the case studies published.

Exercise:
Explain the evolution of .NET framework?
Explain the different components of .NET framework?
What is the role of CLR in .NET?
Write a note on Assemblies and Metadata?
Explain the features of .NET?
Explain the portability features for .Net applications?
Explain the role of .NET in developing the web services?

6

PERL

What Is Perl?

Perl is a free, open source programming language created by Larry Wall. Perl aims for adjectives like "practical" and "quick" and not so much words like "structured" or "elegant". A culture has built up around Perl where people create and give away modules, documentation, sample code, and a thousand other useful things -- visit the Comprehensive Perl Archive Network (CPAN), http://www.cpan.org/, or http://www.perl.com/ to see the amazing range of Perl material available.

Perl is probably best known for text processing -- dealing with files, strings, and regular expressions. However, Perl's quick, informal style makes it attractive for all sorts of little programs. If I need a 23 line program to get some task done, I can write it in Perl and be done in 3
minutes. Perl code is very portable -- I frequently move Perl programs back and forth from the Mac to various Unixes and it just works. With Perl, you are not locked in to any particular vendor or operating system. Perl code is also robust; Perl programs can have bugs, but they will not crash randomly like C or C++ programs. On the other hand, in my opinion, Perl's easy-going style makes it less appealing for large projects where I would rather use Java.

Perl is famous for allowing you to write solutions to complex problems with very short, terse phrases of code. There's something satisfying about reducing a whole computation down to a single line of dense code. However, I never do that. I write Perl code in a boring, straightforward way which tends to spell out what it's actually doing step by step. The terse style is mentioned briefly in the Terse Perl section. Also, in versions 5 and 6, Perl has accumulated more sophisticated features which are not covered here. We just do simple old Perl code.

Running Perl

A Perl program is just a text file. You edit the text of your Perl program, and the Perl interpreter reads that text file directly to "run" it. This structure makes your edit-run-debug cycle nice and fast. On Unix, the Perl interpreter is called "perl" and you run a Perl program by running the Perl interpreter and telling it which file contains your Perl program...

> perl myprog.pl

The interpreter makes one pass of the file to analyze it and if there are no syntax or other obvious errors, the interpreter runs the Perl code. There is no "main" function -- the interpreter just executes the statements in the file starting at the top.

Advanced Web Tehnologies

Following the Unix convention, the very first line in a Perl file usually looks like this...

#!/usr/bin/perl -w

This special line is a hint to Unix to use the Perl interpreter to execute the code in this file. The "-w" switch turns on warnings which is generally a good idea. In unix, use "chmod" to set the execute bit on a Perl file so it can be run right from the prompt...

chmod u+x foo.pl ## set the "execute" bit for the file once

> foo.pl   ## automatically uses the perl interpreter to "run" this file

The second line in a Perl file is usually a "require" declaration that specifies what version of Perl the program expects...

#!/usr/bin/perl -w
require 5.004;

Perl is available for every operating system imaginable, including of course Windows and MacOS, and it's part of the default install in Mac OSX. See the "ports" section of http://www.cpan.org/ to get Perl for a particular system.

Syntax And Variables

The simplest Perl variables are "scalar" variables which hold a single string or number. Scalar variable names begin with a dollar sign ($) such as $sum or $greeting. Scalar and other variables do not need to be pre-declared -- using a variable automatically declares it as a global variable. Variable names and other identifiers are composed of letters, digits, and underscores (_) and are case sensitive. Comments begin with a "#" and extend to the end of the line.

$x = 2; ## scalar var $x set to the number 2
$greeting = "hello"; ## scalar var $greeting set to the string "hello"

A variable that has not been given a value has the special value "undef" which can be detected using the "defined" operator. Undef looks like 0 when used as a number, or the empty string "" when used as a string, although a well written program probably should not depend on undef in that way. When Perl is run with "warnings" enabled (the -w flag), using an undef variable prints a warning.

if (!defined($binky))
{
print "the variable 'binky' has not been given a value!\n";
}

Advanced Web Tehnologies

What's With This '$' Stuff?

Larry Wall, Perl's creator, has a background in linguistics which explains a few things about Perl. I saw a Larry Wall talk where he gave a sort of explanation for the '$' syntax in Perl: In human languages, it's intuitive for each part of speech to have its own sound pattern. So for example, a baby might learn that English nouns end in "-y" -- "mommy," "daddy," "doggy". (It's natural for a baby to over generalize the "rule" to get made up words like "bikey" and "blanky".) In some small way, Perl tries to capture the different-signature-for-different-role pattern in its syntax -- all scalar expressions look alike since they all start with '$'.

Strings

Strings constants are enclosed within double quotes (") or in single quotes ('). Strings in double quotes are treated specially -- special directives like \n (newline) and \x20 (hex 20) are expanded. More importantly, a variable, such as $x, inside a double quoted string is evaluated at run-time and the result is pasted into the string. This evaluation of variables into strings is called "interpolation" and it's a great Perl feature. Single quoted (') strings suppress all the special evaluation -- they do not evaluate \n or $x, and they may contain newlines.

$fname = "binky.txt";
$a = "Could not open the file $fname."; ## $fname evaluated and pasted in -- neato!

$b = 'Could not open the file $fname.'; ## single quotes (') do no special evaluation

$a is now "Could not open the file binky.txt."
$b is now "Could not open the file $fname."

The characters '$' and '@' are used to trigger interpolation into strings, so those characters need to be escaped with a backslash (\) if you want them in a string. For example:
"nick\@stanford.edu found \$1".

The dot operator (.) concatenates two strings. If Perl has a number or other type when it wants a string, it just silently converts the value to a string and continues. It works the other way too -- a string such as "42" will evaluate to the integer 42 in an integer context.

$num = 42;
$string = "The " . $num . " ultimate" . " answer";

$string is now "The 42 ultimate answer"

The operators eq (equal) and ne (not equal) compare two strings. Do not use == to compare strings; use == to compare numbers.

Advanced Web Tehnologies

```
$string = "hello";
($string eq ("hell" . "o"))     ==> TRUE
($string eq "HELLO")            ==> FALSE

$num = 42;
($num-2 == 40)      ==> TRUE
```

The lc("Hello") operator returns the all lower-case version "hello", and uc("Hello") returns the all upper-case version "HELLO".

Fast And Loose Perl

When Perl sees an expression that doesn't make sense, such as a variable that has not been given a value, it tends to just silently pass over the problem and use some default value such as undef. This is better than C or C++ which tend to crash when you do something wrong. Still, you need to be careful with Perl code since it's easy for the language to do something you did not have in mind. Just because Perl code compiles, don't assume it's doing what you intended. Anything compiles in Perl.

Arrays -- @

Array constants are specified using parenthesis ( ) and the elements are separated with commas. Perl arrays are like lists or collections in other languages since they can grow and shrink, but in Perl they are just called "arrays". Array variable names begin with the at-sign (@). Unlike C, the assignment operator (=) works for arrays -- an independent copy of the array and its elements is made. Arrays may not contain other arrays as elements. Perl has sort of a "1-deep" mentality. Actually, it's possible to get around the 1-deep constraint using "references", but it's no fun. Arrays work best if they just contain scalars (strings and numbers). The elements in an array do not all need to be the same type.

```
@array = (1, 2, "hello"); @empty = ();
```

```
## a 3 element array
## the array with 0 elements
```

```
$x = 1;
$y = 2;
@nums = ($x + $y, $x - $y);
```

```
## @nums is now (3, -1)
```

Just as in C, square brackets [ ] are used to refer to elements, so $a[6] is the element at index 6 in the array @a. As in C, array indexes start at 0. Notice that the syntax to access an element begins with '$' not '@' -- use '@' only when referring to the whole array (remember: all scalar expressions begin with $).

@array = (1, 2, "hello", "there"); $array[0] = $array[0] + $array[1];

$array[0] is now 3

Perl arrays are not bounds checked. If code attempts to read an element outside the array size, undef is returned. If code writes outside the array size, the array grows automatically to be big enough. Well written code probably should not rely on either of those features.

@array = (1, 2, "hello", "there");
$sum = $array[0] + $array[27]; ## $sum is now 1, since $array[27] returned undef

$array[99] = "the end";   ## array grows to be size 100

When used in a scalar context, an array evaluates to its length. The "scalar" operator will force the evaluation of something in a scalar context, so you can use scalar() to get the length of an array. As an alternative to using scalar, the expression $#array is the index of the last element of the array which is always one less than the length.

@array = (1, 2, "hello", "there");
$len = @array;   ## $len is now 4 (the length of @array)
$len = scalar(@array)
scalar

same as above, since $len represented a
context anyway, but this is more explicit

@letters = ("a", "b", "c"); $i = $#letters;

$i is now 2

That scalar(@array) is the way to refer to the length of an array is not a great moment in the history of readable code. At least I haven't showed you the even more vulgar forms such as (0 + @a).

The sort operator (sort @a) returns a copy of the array sorted in ascending alphabetic order.
Note that sort does not change the original array. Here are some common ways to sort...

(sort @array) ## sort alphabetically, with

Essential Perl
uppercase first
(sort {$a <=> $b} @array)
(sort {$b cmp $a} @array)
(sort {lc($a) cmp lc($b)} @array)

(somewhat inefficient)

sort numerically
sort reverse alphabetically
sort alphabetically, ignoring case

The sort expression above pass a comparator function {...} to the sort operator, where the special variables $a and $b are the two elements to compare -- cmp is the built-in string compare, and <=> is the built-in numeric compare.

There's a variant of array assignment that is used sometimes to assign several variables at once. If an array on the left hand side of an assignment operation contains the names of variables, the variables are assigned the corresponding values from the right hand side.

($x, $y, $z) = (1, 2, "hello", 4);

assigns $x=1, $y=2, $z="hello", and the 4 is discarded

This type of assignment only works with scalars. If one of the values is an array, the wrong thing happens (see "flattening" below).

Array Add/Remove/Splice Functions

These handy operators will add or remove an element from an array. These operators change the array they operate on...

Operating at the "front" ($array[0]) end of the array...
shift(array) -- returns the frontmost element and removes it from the array. Can be used in a loop to gradually remove and examine all the elements in an array left to right. The foreach operator, below, is another way to examine all the elements.

unshift(array, elem) -- inserts an element at the front of the array.

Opposite of shift.
Operating at the "back" ($array[$len-1]) end of the array...
pop(array) -- returns the endmost element (right hand side) and removes it from the array.

push(array, elem) -- adds a single element to the end of the array. Opposite of pop.

splice(array, index, length, array2) -- removes the section of the array defined by index and length, and replaces that section with the elements from array2. If array2 is omitted, splice() simply deletes. For example, to delete the element at index $i from an array, use splice(@array, $i, 1).

Hash Arrays -- %

Hash arrays, also known as "associative" arrays, are a built-in key/value data structure. Hash arrays are optimized to find the value for a key very quickly. Hash array variables begin with a percent sign (%) and use curly braces { } to access the value for a particular key. If there is no such key in the array, the value returned is undef. The keys are case sensitive, so you may want to consistently uppercase or lowercase strings before using them as a key (use lc and uc).

```
$dict{"bart"}  = "I didn't do it";
$dict{"homer"} = "D'Oh";
$dict{"lisa"}  = "";
```

%dict now contains the key/value pairs (("bart" => "I didn't do it"), ("homer" => "D'oh"), ("lisa" => ""))

```
$string = $dict{"bart"};
```

```
## Lookup the key "bart" to get ## the value "I didn't do it"
$string = $dict{"marge"};
## Returns undef -- there is no entry for "marge"
```

```
$dict{"homer"} = "Mmmm, scalars";
```

```
## change the value for the key ## "homer" to "Mmmm, scalars"
```

A hash array may be converted back and forth to an array where each key is immediately followed by its value. Each key is adjacent to its value, but the order of the key/value pairs depends on the hashing of the keys and so appears random. The "keys" operator returns an array of the keys from an associative array. The "values" operator returns an array of all the values, in an order consistent with the keys operator.

```
@array = %dict;
```

```
@array will look something like
("homer", "D'oh", "lisa", "", "bart", "I didn't do it");
```

```
(keys %dict) looks like ("homer", "lisa, "bart")
or use (sort (keys %dict))
```

You can use => instead of comma and so write a hash array value this cute way...

```
%dict = (
"bart" => "I didn't do it",
"homer" => "D'Oh",
"lisa" => "",
);
```

Advanced Web Tehnologies

In Java or C you might create an object or struct to gather a few items together. In Perl you might just throw those things together in a hash array.

@ARGV and %ENV

The built-in array @ARGV contains the command line arguments for a Perl program. The following run of the Perl program critic.pl will have the ARGV array ("-poetry", "poem.txt").

unix% perl critic.pl -poetry poem.txt %ENV contains the environment variables of the context that launched the Perl program.
@ARGV and %ENV make the most sense in a Unix environment.

If/While Syntax

Perl's control syntax looks like C's control syntax . Blocks of statements are surrounded by curly braces { }. Statements are terminated with semicolons (;). The parenthesis and curly braces are required in if/while/for forms. There is not a distinct "boolean" type, and there are no "true" or "false" keywords in the language. Instead, the empty string, the empty array, the number 0 and undef all evaluate to false, and everything else is true. The logical operators &&, ||, ! work as in C. There are also keyword equivalents (and, or, not) which are almost the same, but have lower precedence.

IF

```
if (expr)
{
stmt;
stmt;
## basic if -- ( ) and { } required
}


if (expr)
{
stmt;
stmt;
## if + elsif + else
}
elsif (expr)
{
stmt;
stmt;
## note the strange spelling of "elsif"
}
else
{
```

```
stmt;
stmt;
}


unless (expr)
{
stmt;
stmt;
## if variant which negates the boolean test
}
```

If Variants

As an alternative to the classic if() { } structure, you may use if, while, and unless as modifiers that come after the single statement they control...

$x = 3 if $x > 3;   ## equivalent to: if ($x > 3) { $x = 3; }

$x = 3 unless $x <= 3;
For these constructs, the parentheses are not required around the boolean expression. This may be another case where Perl is using a structure from human languages. I never use this syntax because I just cannot get used to seeing the condition after the statement it modifies. If you were defusing a bomb, would you like instructions like this: "Locate the red wire coming out of the control block and cut it. Unless it's a weekday -- in that case cut the black wire."

Loops

These work just as in C...

```
while (expr)
{
stmt;
stmt;
}

for (init_expr ; test_expr ; increment_expr )
{
stmt;
stmt;
}
```

typical for loop to count 0..99 for ($i=0; $i<100; $i++)
```
{
stmt; stmt;
}
```

The "next" operator forces the loop to the next iteration. The "last" operator breaks out of the loop like break in C. This is one case where Perl (last) does not use the same keyword name as C (break).

Array Iteration — foreach

The "foreach" construct is a handy way to iterate a variable over all the elements in an array. Because of foreach, you rarely need to write a traditional for or while loop to index into an array. Foreach is also likely to be implemented efficiently. (It's a shame Java does not include a compact iteration syntax in the language. It would make Java a better language at the cost of some design elegance.)

```
foreach $var (@array)
{
stmt;   ## use $var in here
stmt;
}
```

Any array expression may be used in the foreach. The array expression is evaluated once before the loop starts. The iterating variable, such as $var, is actually a pointer to each element in the array, so assigning to $var will actually change the elements in the array.

File Input

Variables which represent files are called "file handles", and they are handled differently from other variables. They do not begin with any special character -- they are just plain words. By convention, file handle variables are written in all upper case, like FILE_OUT or SOCK. The file handles are all in a global namespace, so you cannot allocate them locally like other variables. File handles can be passed from one routine to another like strings (detailed below).

The standard file handles STDIN, STDOUT, and STDERR are automatically opened before the program runs. Surrounding a file handle with <> is an expression that returns one line from the file including the "\n" character, so <STDIN> returns one line from standard input. The <> operator returns undef when there is no more input. The "chop" operator removes the last character from a string, so it can be used just after an input operation to remove the trailing "\n". The "chomp" operator is similar, but only removes the character if it is the end-of-line character.

```
$line = <STDIN>; chomp($line);
```

read one line from the STDIN file handle ## remove the trailing "\n" if present

```
$line2 = <FILE2>;
```

read one line from the FILE2 file handle ## which must be have been opened previously

Since the input operator returns undef at the end of the file, the standard pattern to read all the lines in a file is...

read every line of a file while ($line = <STDIN>) {
do something with $line
}

Open and Close

The "open" and "close" operators operate as in C to connect a file handle to a filename in the file system.

open(F1, "filename");
F1
open(F2, ">filename");
F2
open(F3, ">>appendtome")

close(F1);

open "filename" for reading as file handle ## open "filename" for writing as file handle ## open "appendtome" for appending ## close a file handle

Open can also be used to establish a reading or writing connection to a separate process launched by the OS. This works best on Unix.

open(F4, "ls -l |"); open(F5, "| mail $addr");

open a pipe to read from an ls process ## open a pipe to write to a mail process
Passing commands to the shell to launch an OS process in this way can be very convenient, but
it's also a famous source of security problems in CGI programs. When writing a CGI, do not pass a string from the client side as a filename in a call to open().

Open returns undef on failure, so the following phrase is often to exit if a file can't be opened. The die operator prints an error message and terminates the program.

open(FILE, $fname) || die "Could not open $fname\n";

In this example, the logical-or operator || essentially builds an if statement, since it only evaluates the second expression if the first if false. This construct is a little strange, but it is a common code pattern for Perl error handling.

Input Variants

In a scalar context the input operator reads one line at a time. In an array context, the input operator reads the entire file into memory as an array of its lines...

Advanced Web Tehnologies

```
@a = <FILE>; ## read the whole file in as an array of lines
```

This syntax can be dangerous. The following statement looks like it reads just a single line, but actually the left hand side is an array context, so it reads the whole file and then discards all but the first line....

```
my($line) = <FILE>;
```

The behavior of <FILE> also depends on the special global variable $/ which is the current the end-of-line marker (usually "\n"). Setting $/ to undef causes <FILE> to read the whole file into a single string.

```
$/ = undef;
$all = <FILE>;
```

```
## read the whole file into one string
```

You can remember that $/ is the end-of-line marker because "/" is used to designate separate lines of poetry. I thought this mnemonic was silly when I first saw it, but sure enough, I now remember that $/ is the end-of-line marker.

Print Output

Print takes a series of things to print separated by commas. By default, print writes to the STDOUT file handle.

```
print "Woo Hoo\n";   ## print a string to STDOUT
```

```
$num = 42;
$str = " Hoo";
print "Woo", $a, " bbb $num", "\n";  ## print several things
```
An optional first argument to print can specify the destination file handle. There is no comma after the file handle, but I always forget to omit it.

```
print FILE "Here", " there", " everywhere!", "\n"; ## no comma after FILE
```

File Processing Example

As an example, here's some code that opens each of the files listed in the @ARGV array, and reads in and prints out their contents to standard output...

```
#!/usr/bin/perl -w
require 5.004;
```

Open each command line file and print its contents to standard out foreach $fname (@ARGV)
{

```
open(FILE, $fname) || die("Could not open $fname\n");
while($line = <FILE>)
{
print $line;
}
close(FILE);
}
```

The above uses "die" to abort the program if one of the files cannot be opened. We could use a more flexible strategy where we print an error message for that file but continue to try to process the other files. Alternately we could use the function call exit(-1) to exit the program with an error code. Also, the following shift pattern is a common alternative way to iterate through an array...

```
while($fname = shift(@ARGV)) {...
```

String Processing with Regular Expressions

Perl's most famous strength is in string manipulation with regular expressions. Perl has a million string processing features -- we'll just cover the main ones here. The simple syntax to search for a pattern in a string is...

($string =~ /pattern/) ## true if the pattern is found somewhere in the string

```
("binky" =~ /ink/)    ==> TRUE
("binky" =~ /onk/)    ==> FALSE
```
In the simplest case, the exact characters in the regular expression pattern must occur in the string somewhere. All of the characters in the pattern must be matched, but the pattern does not need to be right at the start or end of the string, and the pattern does not need to use all the characters in the string.

Character Codes

The power of regular expressions is that they can specify patterns, not just fixed characters. First, there are special matching characters...

 a, X, 9 -- ordinary characters just match that character exactly
 . (a period) -- matches any single character except "\n"
 \w -- (lowercase w) matches a "word" character: a letter or digit [a-zA-Z0-9]
 \W -- (uppercase W) any non word character
 \s -- (lowercase s) matches a single whitespace character -- space, newline, return, tab, form [\n\r\t\f]
 \S -- (uppercase S) any non whitespace character \t, \n, \r -- tab, newline, return
 \d -- decimal digit [0-9] \ -- inhibit the "specialness" of a character. So, for example, use \. to match a period or \\ to match a slash. If you are unsure if a character has special meaning, such as '@', you can always put a slash in front of it \@ to make sure it is treated just as a character.

Advanced Web Tehnologies

"piiig" =~ /p...g/
==> TRUE
. = any char (except \n)

"piiig" =~ /.../
==> TRUE
need not use up the whole string

"piiig" =~ /p....g/
==> FALSE
must use up the whole pattern (the g is not matched)

"piiig" =~ /p\w\w\wg/
==> TRUE
\w = any letter or digit

"p123g" =~ /p\d\d\dg/
==> TRUE
\d = 0..9 digit

The modifier "i" after the last / means the match should be case insensitive...

"PiIIg" =~ "PiIIg" =~
/pIiig/ /pIiig/i

==> FALSE
==> TRUE

String interpolation works in regular expression patterns. The variable values are pasted into the expression once before it is evaluated. Characters like * and + continue to have their special meanings in the pattern after interpolation, unless the pattern is bracketed with a \Q..\E. The following examples test if the pattern in $target occurs within brackets < > in $string...

$string =~ /<$target>/ ## Look for <$target>, '.' '*' keep their special meanings in $target

$string =~ /<\Q$target\E>/ ## The \Q..\E puts a backslash in front of every char,
so '.' '*' etc. in $target will not have
their special meanings

Similar to the \Q..\E form, the quotemeta() function returns a string with every character \ escaped. There is an optional "m" (for "match") that comes before the first /. If the "m" is used, then any character can be used for the delimiter instead of / -- so you could use " or # to delimit the pattern. This is handy if what you are

trying to match has a lot of /'s in it. If the delimiter is the single quote (') then interpolation is suppressed. The following expressions are all equivalent...

Advanced Web Tehnologies

"piiig" =~ m/piiig/
"piiig" =~ m"piiig"
"piiig" =~ m#piiig#

Control Codes

Things get really interesting when you add in control codes to the regular expression pattern...

? -- match 0 or 1 occurrences of the pattern to its left
* -- 0 or more occurrences of the pattern to its left
+ -- 1 or more occurrences of the pattern to its left
| -- (vertical bar) logical or -- matches the pattern either on its left or right
parenthesis ( ) -- group sequences of patterns
^ -- matches the start of the string
$ -- matches the end of the string

Leftmost & Largest

First, Perl tries to find the leftmost match for the pattern, and second it tries to use up as much of the string as possible -- i.e. let + and * use up as many characters as possible.

Regular Expression Examples

The following series gradually demonstrate each of the above control codes. Study them carefully
small details in regular expressions make a big difference. That's what makes them powerful, but it makes them tricky as well.

Old joke: What do you call a pig with three eyes? Piiig!

Search for the pattern 'iiig' in the string 'piiig' "piiig" =~ m/iiig/ ==> TRUE

The pattern may be anywhere inside the string "piiig" =~ m/iii/ ==> TRUE

All of the pattern must match
"piiig" =~ m/iiii/ ==> FALSE

. = any char but \n "piiig" =~ m/...ig/ ==> TRUE

"piiig" =~ m/p.i../ ==> TRUE

The last . in the pattern is not matched "piiig" =~ m/p.i.../ ==> FALSE

\d = digit [0-9]
"p123g" =~ m/p\d\d\dg/ ==> TRUE

"p123g" =~ m/p\d\d\d\d/ ==> FALSE
\w = letter or digit "p123g" =~ m/\w\w\w\w\w/ ==> TRUE

i+ = one or more i's "piiig" =~ m/pi+g/ ==> TRUE

matches iii
"piiig" =~ m/i+/ ==> TRUE

"piiig" =~ m/p+i+g+/ ==> TRUE

"piiig" =~ m/p+g+/ ==> FALSE

i* = zero or more i's "piiig" =~ m/pi*g/ ==> TRUE

"piiig" =~ m/p*i*g*/ ==> TRUE

X* can match zero X's "piiig" =~ m/pi*X*g/ ==> TRUE

^ = start, $ = end "piiig" =~ m/^pi+g$/ ==> TRUE

i is not at the start "piiig" =~ m/^i+g$/ ==> FALSE

i is not at the end
"piiig" =~ m/^pi+$/ ==> FALSE

"piiig" =~ m/^p.+g$/ ==> TRUE

"piiig" =~ m/^p.+$/ ==> TRUE

"piiig" =~ m/^.+$/ ==> TRUE

g is not at the start "piiig" =~ m/^g.+$/ ==> FALSE

Needs at least one char after the g "piiig" =~ m/g.+/ ==> FALSE

Needs at least zero chars after the g "piiig" =~ m/g.*/ ==> TRUE

| = left or right expression
"cat" =~ m/^(cat|hat)$/ ==> TRUE

"hat" =~ m/^(cat|hat)$/ ==> TRUE
"cathatcatcat" =~ m/^(cat|hat)+$/ ==> TRUE
"cathatcatcat" =~ m/^(c|a|t|h)+$/ ==> TRUE
"cathatcatcat" =~ m/^(c|a|t)+$/ ==> FALSE

Matches and stops at first 'cat'; does not get to 'catcat' on the right "cathatcatcat"
=~ m/(c|a|t)+/ ==> TRUE

? = optional
"12121x2121x2"   =~   m/^(1x?2)+$/   ==>   TRUE   "aaaxbbbabaxbb"   =~
m/^(a+x?b+)+$/ ==> TRUE "aaaxxbbb" =~ m/^(a+x?b+)+$/ ==> FALSE ####
Three words separated by spaces
"Easy does it" =~ m/^\w+\s+\w+\s+\w+$/ ==> TRUE

Just   matches   "gates@microsoft"   --   \w   does   not   match   the   "."
"bill.gates@microsoft.com" =~ m/\w+@\w+/ ==> TRUE

Add   the   .'s   to   get   the   whole   thing   "bill.gates@microsoft.com"   =~
m/^(\w|\.)+@(\w|\.)+$/ ==> TRUE

words separated by commas and possibly spaces
"Klaatu,   barada,nikto" =~ m/^\w+(,\s*\w+)*$/ ==> TRUE

Character Classes

Square brackets can be used to represent a set of characters. For example
[aeiouAEIOU] is a one character pattern that matches a vowel. Most characters
are not special inside a square bracket and so can be used without a leading
backslash (\). \w, \s, and \d work inside a character class, and the dash (-) can be
used to express a range of characters, so [a-z] matches lowercase "a" through "z".
So the \w code is equivalent to [a-zA-Z0-9]. If the first character in a character
class is a caret (^) the set is inverted, and matches all the characters not in the
given set. So [^0-9] matches all characters that are not digits.

The parts of an email address on either side of the "@" are made up of letters,
numbers plus dots, underbars, and dashes. As a character class that's just [\w._-].

"bill.gates_emporer@microsoft.com" =~ m/^[\w._-]+@[\w._-]+$/ ==> TRUE

Match Variables

If a =~ match expression is true, the special variables $1, $2, ... will be the
substrings that matched parts of the pattern in parenthesis -- $1 matches the
first left parenthesis, $2 the second left parenthesis, and so on. The following
pattern picks out three words separated by whitespace...

if ("this and that" =~ /(\w+)\s+(\w+)\s+(\w+)/)
{
if the above matches, $1=="this", $2=="and", $3=="that"
This is a nice way to parse a string -- write a regular expression for the pattern
you expect putting parenthesis around the parts you want to pull out. Only use $1,

Advanced Web Tehnologies

$2, etc. when the if =~ returns true. Other regular-expression systems use \1 and

\2 instead of $1 $2, and Perl supports that syntax as well. There are three other special variables: $& (dollar-ampersand) = the matched string, $` (dollar-back-quote) = the string before what was matched, and $' (dollar-quote) = the string following what was matched.

The following loop rips through a string and pulls out all the email addresses. It demonstrates using a character class, using $1 etc. to pull out parts of the match string, and using $' after the match.

$str = 'blah blah nick@cs.stanford.edu, blah blah balh billg@microsoft.com blah blah';

```
while ($str =~ /(([\w._-]+)\@([\w._-]+))/)
{
## look for an email addr
print "user:$2 host:$3   all:$1\n";        ## parts of the addr
$str = $';           ## set the str to be the "rest" of the string
}
```

output:

user:nick   host:cs.stanford.edu   all:nick@cs.stanford.edu   user:billg host:microsoft.com all:billg@microsoft.com

Substitution

A slight variation of the match operator can be used to search and replace. Put an "s" in front of the pattern and follow the match pattern with a replacement pattern.

Change all "is" strings to "is not" -- a sure way to improve any document
$str =~ s/is/is not/ig;

The replacement pattern can use $1, $2 to refer to parts of the matched string. The "g" modifier after the last / means do the replacement repeatedly in the target string. The modifier "i" means the match should not be case sensitive. The following example finds instances of the letter "r" or "l" followed by a word character, and replaces that pattern with "w" followed by the same word character. Sounds like Tweety Bird...

Change "r" and "l" followed by a word char to "w" followed
by the same word char

$x = "This dress exacerbates the genetic betrayal that is my Legacy.\n"; $x =~ s/(r|l)(\w)/w$2/ig; ## r or l followed by a word char
$x is now "This dwess exacewbates the genetic betwayal that is my wegacy."

The ? Trick

One problem with * and +, is that they are "greedy" -- they try to use up as many characters as

Perl   Page: 121

they can. Suppose you are trying to pick out all of the characters between two curly braces { }.
The simplest thing would be to use the pattern...

m/{(.*)}/   -- pick up all the characters between {}'s

The problem is that if you match against the string "{group 1} xx {group 2}", the * will aggressively run right over the first } and match the second }. So $1 will be "group 1} xx {group 2" instead of "group 1". Fortunately Perl has a nice solution to the too-aggressive-*/+ problem. If a ? immediately follows the * or +, then it tries to find the shortest repetition which works instead of the longest. You need the ? variant most often when matching with .* or \S* which can easily use up more than you had in mind. Use ".*?" to skip over stuff you don't care about, but have something you do care about immediately to its right. Such as..

m/{(.*?)}/ ## pick up all the characters between {}'s, but stop ## at the first }

The old way to skip everything up until a certain character, say }, uses the [^}] construct like this...

m/{([^}]*)}/ ## the inner [^}] matches any char except }

I prefer the (.*?) form. In fact, I suspect it was added to the language precisely as an improvement over the [^}]* form.

Substring

The index(string, string-to-look-for, start-index) operator searches the first string starting at the given index for an occurrence of the second string. Returns the 0 based index of the first occurrence, or -1 if not found. The following code uses index() to walk through a string and count the number of times "binky" occurs.

```
$count = 0;
$pos = 0;

while ( ($pos = index($string, "binky", $pos) != -1)
{
$count++;
$pos++;
}
```

The function substr(string, index, length) pulls a substring out of the given string. Substr() starts at the given index and continues for the given length.

Split

The split operator takes a regular expression, and a string, and returns an array of all the substrings from the original string which were separated by that regular expression. The following example pulls out words separated by commas possibly with whitespace thrown in...

```
split(/\s*,\s*/, "dress ,betrayal, legacy") ## returns the array
```

```
("dress", "betrayal", "legacy")
```

Split is often a useful way to pull an enumeration out of some text for processing. If the number -1 is passed as a third argument to split, then it will interpret an instance of the separator pattern at the end of the string as marking a last, empty element (note the comma after the last word)...

```
split(/\s*,\s*/, "dress , betrayal , legacy,", -1) ## returns the array
```

```
("dress", "betrayal", "legacy", "")
```

Character Translate -- tr

The tr// operator goes through a string and replaces characters with other characters.

```
$string =~ tr/a/b/;   -- change all a's to b's
$string =~ tr/A-Z/a-z/; -- change uppercase to lowercase      (actually lc()
is better for this)
```

Subroutines

Perl subroutines encapsulate blocks of code in the usual way. You do not need to define subroutines before they are used, so Perl programs generally have their "main" code first, and their subroutines laid out toward the bottom of the file. A subroutine can return a scalar or an array.

```
$x = Three(); exit(0);
## call to Three() returns 3
## exit the program normally

sub Three
{
return (1 + 2);
}
```

Advanced Web Tehnologies

Local Variables and Parameters

Historically, many Perl programs leave all of their variables global. It's especially convenient since the variables do not need to be declared. This "quick 'n dirty" style does not scale well when trying to write larger programs. With Perl 5, the "my" construct allows one or more variables to be declared. (Older versions of perl had a "local" construct which should be avoided.)

```
my $a; ## declare $a
my $b = "hello"        ## declare $b, and assign it "hello"
my @array = (1, 2, 3);        ## declare @array and assign it (1, 2, 3)
my ($x, $y);  ## declare $x and $y
my ($a, $b) = (1, "hello");    ## declare $a and $b, and assign $a=1,
$b="hello"
```

The "my" construct is most often used to declare local varaiables in a subroutine...

```
sub Three
{
my ($x, $y);   # declare vars $x and $y
$x = 1;
$y = 2;
return ($x + $y);
}
```

Variant of Three() which inits $x and $y with the array trick sub Three2
```
{
my ($x, $y) = (1, 2); return ($x + $y);
}
```

@_ Parameters

Perl subroutines do not have formal named parameters like other languages. Instead, all the parameters are passed in a single array called "@_". The elements in @_ actually point to the original caller-side parameters, so the called function is responsible for making copies. Usually the subroutine will pull the values out of @_ and copy them to local variables. A Sum() function which takes two numbers and adds them looks like...

```
sub Sum1
{
my ($x, $y) = @_; # the first lines of many functions look like this
# to retrieve and name their params
return($x + $y);
}
```

Variant where you pull the values out of @_ directly
This avoids copying the parameters
```perl
sub Sum2
{
return($_[0] + $_[1]);
}
```

How Sum() would really be written in Perl -- it takes an array
of numbers of arbitrary length, and adds all of them...
```perl
sub Sum3
{
my ($sum, $elem); # declare local vars
$sum = 0;
foreach $elem (@_)
{
$sum += $elem;
}
return($sum);
}
```

Variant of above using shift instead of foreach sub sum4 {
```perl
my ($sum, $elem); $sum = 0;

while(defined($elem = shift(@_)))
{
$sum += $elem;
}
return($sum);
}
```

File Handle Arguments

The file handles are all in a global namespace, so you cannot allocate them
locally like other variables. File handles can be passed from one routine to
another like strings, but this amounts to just passing around references to a
single global file handle...

```perl
open(FILE, ">file.txt");
SayHello("FILE");
close(FILE);
```

Here, the file handle FILE is passed as the string "FILE" sub SayHello
```perl
{
my($file_handle) = @_;
```
Prints to the file handle identified in $file_handle print $file_handle "I'm a little
teapot, short and stout.\n";
```perl
}
```

Actually, the file handle doesn't even need to be quoted in the call, so the above call could be written as SayHello(FILE);. This is the "bareword" feature of Perl where a group of characters that does not have another syntactic interpretation is passed through as if it were a string. I prefer not to rely on barewords, so I write the call as SayHello("FILE");.

Returning Multiple Values to the Caller

How to communicate back to the caller? Returning a single value to the caller works great when that's all you need. What about the case where there are multiple pieces of information to communicate back to the caller? The subroutine could communicate by modifying actual arguments in @_ , but that gets ugly. A better approach is to pack multiple things into an array and return that. The caller can catch the return array and use it as an array, or assign it to a my() expression that puts the values into named variables...

```
Suppose this function returns a (num, string) array
where the num is a result code and the string is
the human readable form
sub DoSomething
{
# does something
return(-13, "Core Breach Imminent!!"); # return an array len 2
}

# so a call would look like...
my ($num, $string) = DoSomething();
if ($num<0)
{
print "Panic:$string\n";
}
```

The values returned must be scalars — if they themselves are arrays, they will be flattened into the return array which is probably not what you want.

Flattened Arguments

Perl arrays are always "1-deep" or "flat". The arguments into a function all get "flattened" into the single @_ array, so it is not possible to pass an array as one of several arguments since it gets flattened out with the other arguments...

```
Sum3(1, 2, (3, 4));
## returns 10 -- the arg array is flattened to (1, 2, 3, 4)
```

This flattening can hurt you if you try to assign to an element which is an array...

```
my(@nums, $three) = ((1, 2), 3);
```

You might think that this assigns (1, 2) to @nums and 3 to $three. But instead the right hand side gets flattened to (1, 2, 3) which is then assigned to @nums, and $three does not get a value. Only use the my($x, $y) = (...); form when assigning a bunch of scalar values. If any of the values are arrays, then you should separate out all the assignments, each on its own line...

```
my (@array, $x);
@array = ...;
$x = ...;
```

You can get around the 1-deep by storing references to arrays in other arrays – see the References section.

Global Vars and 'use strict'

You need to be careful to keep local and global variables straight, since by default, the compiler does not warn about possibly erroneous code. Suppose a subroutine has a $string local variable, except it is mistyped as $strning in one place. By default, this just declares a global variable named $strning.

Each of the following declarations causes Perl to enforce bug-reducing rules.

use strict 'vars'; use strict;

```
## enforce local/global var declarations
## like above, but with some additional style checks
```
With strict vars, variables inside functions must be declared with my(). Variables which are intended to be global must be referred to with two colons (::) in front of their name or must be declared with a global my(). Violating these rules results in a compile-time error.

With strict vars...

1. Undeclared global vars must begin with "::" at all times $::global = 13;

2. Or a global may be declared with a my(), in which case
the :: is not necessary
my $global2 = 42;

```
sub foo
{
my $sum;
$sum = $::global + $global2;
$sum and $global2 work without extra syntax return($sum);
}
```

Both the "-w" option and "use strict" are good ideas or any Perl program larger than a page or two in size. Without them, you will inevitably waste time debugging some trivial variable name mixup or syntax error.

Running External Programs

Perl can be used to invoke other programs and mess with their input and output. The most straightforward way to do this is with the system function which takes a command line string (or an array of strings), and has the operating system try to run it (this makes the most sense in a Unix environment). System returns 0 when the program successfully completes, or on error the global variable $? should be set to an error description.

```
system("mail nick < tmp.txt") == 0 | die "system error $?";
```

The file-open function can also be used to run a program -- a vertical var (|) at the end of the filename runs the filename as a process, and lets you read from its output...

```
open(F, "ls -l |");
```

run the ls -l process, and name its

output F

```
while (defined($line = <F>)) {
## read F, line by line
...
```

The same trick works for writing to a process -- just put the vertical bar at the beginning. Writing on the file handle goes to the standard input of the process. On Unix, the mail program can take the body of an email message as standard input...

```
$user = "nick\@cs";
$subject = "mail from perl";

open(MAIL, "| mail -s $subject $user"); print(MAIL, "Here's some email for you\n");
print(MAIL, "blah blah blah, ....");
close(MAIL);
```

If a programmer ever uses this technique to send Spam email, then all the other programmers will hunt that programmer down and explain the tragedy of the commons to them before the traditional beheading. Also, when writing a CGI, it's important that you control the sorts of strings that are passed to system functions like open() and system(). Do not take text from the user and pass it directory to a call to system() or open() – the text must be checked to avoid errors and security problems.

References

I'm happiest writing Perl code that does not use references because they always give me a mild headache. Here's the short version of how they work. The backslash operator (\) computes a reference to something. The reference is a scalar that points to the original thing. The '$' dereferences to access the original thing.

Suppose there is a string...

$str = "hello"; ## original string

And there is a reference that points to that string...

$ref = \$str;   ## compute $ref that points to $str

The expression to access $str is $$ref. Essentially, the alphabetic part of the variable, 'str', is replaced with the dereference expression '$ref'...

print "$$ref\n"; ## prints "hello" -- identical to "$str\n";

Here's an example of the same principle with a reference to an array...

@a = (1, 2, 3);## original array

$aRef = \@a; ## reference to the array

print "a: @a\n";   ## prints "a: 1 2 3"
print "a: @$aRef\n"; ## exactly the same

Curly braces { } can be added in code and in strings to help clarify the stack of @, $, ...

print "a: @{$aRef}\n";   ## use { } for clarity

Here's how you put references to arrays in another array to make it look two dimensional...

@a = (1, 2, 3);
@b = (4, 5, 6);
@root = (\@a, \@b);

print "a: @a\n";

a: (1
2
3)

```
print "a: @{$root[0]}\n";
## a: (1
2
3)

print "b: @{$root[1]}\n";
## b: (4
5
6)

scalar(@root)
## root len ==
2

scalar(@{$root[0]})
## a len: == 3
```

For arrays of arrays, the [ ] operations can stack together so the syntax is more C like...

```
$root[1][0]    ## this is 4
```

Terse Perl

Perl supports a style of coding with very short phrases. For example, many built in functions use the special scalar variable $_ if no other variable is specified. So file reading code...

```
while ($line = <FILE>)
{
print $line;
}
```

Can be written as...

```
while (<FILE>)
{
print;
}
```

It turns out that <FILE> assigns its value into $_ if no variable is specified, and likewise print reads from $_ if nothing is specified. Perl is filled with little shortcuts like that, so many phrases can be written more tersely by omitting explicit variables. I don't especially like the "short" style, since I actually like having named variables in my code, but obviously it depends on personal taste and the goal for the code. If the code is going to be maintained or debugged by someone else in the future, then named variables seem like a good idea.

## 7

WEB APPLICATIONS IN ASP.NET

ASP.NET Coding Modules:

HTTP Modules

HTTP modules are .NET components that implement the System.Web.IHttpModule interface. These components plug themselves into the ASP.NET request processing pipeline by registering themselves for certain events. Whenever those events occur, ASP.NET invokes the interested HTTP modules so that the modules can play with the request.

An HTTP module is supposed to implement the following methods of the IHttpModule interface:

Method Name	Description
Init	This method allows an HTTP module to register its event handlers to the events in the HttpApplication object.
Dispose	This method gives HTTP module an opportunity to perform any clean up before the object gets garbage collected.

An HTTP module can register for the following events exposed by the System.Web.HttpApplication object.

EVENT NAME	DESCRIPTION
AcquireRequestState	This event is raised when ASP.NET runtime is ready to acquire the Session state of the current HTTP request.
AuthenticateRequest	This event is raised when ASP.NET 6runtime is ready to authenticate the identity of the user.
AuthorizeRequest	This event is raised when ASP.NET runtime is ready to authorize the user for the resources user is trying to access.
BeginRequest	This event is raised when ASP.NET runtime receives a new HTTP request.
Disposed	This event is raised when ASP.NET completes the processing of HTTP request.
EndRequest	This event is raised just before sending the response content to the client.

Error	This event is raised when an unhandled exception occurs during the processing of HTTP request.
PostRequestHandlerExecute	This event is raised just after HTTP handler finishes execution.
PreRequestHandlerExecute	This event is raised just before ASP.NET begins executing a handler for the HTTP request. After this event, ASP.NET will forward the request to the appropriate HTTP handler.
PreSendRequestContent	This event is raised just before ASP.NET sends the response contents to the client. This event allows us to change the contents before it gets delivered to the client. We can use this event to add the contents, which are common in all pages, to the page output. For example, a common menu, header or footer.
PreSendRequestHeaders	This event is raised just before ASP.NET sends the HTTP response headers to the client. This event allows us to change the headers before they get delivered to the client. We can use this event to add cookies and custom data into headers.
ReleaseRequestState	This event is raised after ASP.NET finishes executing all request handlers.
ResolveRequestCache	This event is raised to determine whether the request can be fulfilled by returning the contents from the Output Cache. This depends on how the Output Caching has been setup for your web application.
UpdateRequestCache	This event is raised when ASP.NET has completed processing the current HTTP request and the output contents are ready to be added to the Output Cache. This depends on how the Output Caching has been setup for your Web application.

Apart from these events, there are four more events that we can use. We can hook up to these events by implementing the methods in the global.asax file of our Web application.

These events are as follows:
Application_OnStart
This event is raised when the very first request arrives to the
Web application.
Application_OnEnd

This event is raised just before the application is going to terminate.

Session_OnStart

This event is raised for the very first request of the user's session.

Session_OnEnd

This event is raised when the session is abandoned or expired.

Registering HTTP Modules in Configuration Files

Once an HTTP module is built and copied into the bin directory of our Web application or copied into the Global Assembly Cache, then we will register it in either the web.config or machine.config file.

We can use <httpModules> and <add> nodes for adding HTTP modules to our Web applications. In fact the modules are listed by using <add> nodes in between <httpModules> and </httpModules> nodes.

Since configuration settings are inheritable, the child directories inherit configuration settings of the parent directory. As a consequence, child directories might inherit some unwanted HTTP modules as part of the parent configuration; therefore, we need a way to remove those unwanted modules. We can use the <remove> node for this.

If we want to remove all of the inherited HTTP modules from our application, we can use the <clear> node.

The following is a generic example of adding an HTTP module:

```
<httpModules>
<add type="classname, assemblyname"
name="modulename" />
<httpModules>
```

The following is a generic example of removing an HTTP module from your application.

```
<httpModules>
        <remove name="modulename" />
<httpModules>
```

In the above XML,

The type attribute specifies the actual type of the HTTP module in the form of class and assembly name.

The name attribute specifies the friendly name for the module. This is the name that will be used by other applications for identifying the HTTP module.

Use of HTTP Modules by the ASP.NET Runtime

ASP.NET runtime uses HTTP modules for implementing some special features. The following snippet from the machine.config file shows the HTTP modules installed by the
ASP.NET runtime.

```
<httpModules>
<add name="OutputCache"
type="System.Web.Caching.OutputCacheModule"/>
<add name="Session"
type="System.Web.SessionState.SessionStateModule"/>
<add name="WindowsAuthentication"
type="System.Web.Security.WindowsAuthenticationModule"/> <add
name="FormsAuthentication"
type="System.Web.Security.FormsAuthenticationModule"/> <add
name="PassportAuthentication"
type="System.Web.Security.PassportAuthenticationModule"/>
<add name="UrlAuthorization"
type="System.Web.Security.UrlAuthorizationModule"/> <add
name="FileAuthorization"
type="System.Web.Security.FileAuthorizationModule"/>
</httpModules>
```

All of the above HTTP modules are used by ASP.NET to provide services like authentication and authorization, session management and output caching. Since these modules have been registered in machine.config file, these modules are automatically available to all of the Web applications.

Implementing an HTTP Module for Providing Security Services

Now we will implement an HTTP module that provides security services for our Web application. Our HTTP module will basically provide a custom authentication service. It will receive authentication credentials in HTTP request and will determine whether those credentials are valid. If yes, what roles are the user associated with? Through the User.Identity object, it will associate those roles that are accessible to our Web application pages to the user's identity.

Following is the code of our HTTP module.

```
using System;
using System.Web;
using System.Security.Principal;
namespace SecurityModules
```

```
{
<summary>
Summary description for Class1.
</summary>

public class CustomAuthenticationModule : IHttpModule
{
 public CustomAuthenticationModule()
 {
 }
 public void Init(HttpApplication r_objApplication)
 {
 // Register our event handler with Application object.
 r_objApplication.AuthenticateRequest +=
        new EventHandler(this.AuthenticateRequest) ;
 }

 public void Dispose()
 {
 // Left blank because we dont have to do anything.
 }

 private void AuthenticateRequest(object r_objSender, EventArgs
                  r_objEventArgs)
 {
 Authenticate user credentials, and find out user roles.
 HttpApplication objApp = (HttpApplication) r_objSender ;
 HttpContext objContext = (HttpContext) objApp.Context ;
 if ( (objApp.Request["userid"] == null) ||
 (objApp.Request["password"] == null) )
 {
 objContext.Response.Write("<H1>Credentials not provided</H1>")
    ;
 objContext.Response.End() ;
 }
 string userid = "" ;
 userid = objApp.Request["userid"].ToString() ;
 string password = "" ;
 password = objApp.Request["password"].ToString() ;
 string[] strRoles ;
 strRoles = AuthenticateAndGetRoles(userid, password) ;
 if ((strRoles == null) || (strRoles.GetLength(0) == 0))
 {
 objContext.Response.Write("<H1>We are sorry but we could not find this user id
     and password in our database</H1>") ;
 objApp.CompleteRequest() ;
 }
```

```
GenericIdentity objIdentity = new GenericIdentity(userid,
                        "CustomAuthentication") ;
  objContext.User = new GenericPrincipal(objIdentity, strRoles)
}

  private string[] AuthenticateAndGetRoles(string r_strUserID, string
                        r_strPassword)
 {
  string[] strRoles = null ;
  if ((r_strUserID.Equals("Steve")) &&
                        (r_strPassword.Equals("15seconds")))
  {
  strRoles = new String[1] ;
  strRoles[0] = "Administrator" ;
  }
  else if ((r_strUserID.Equals("Mansoor")) &&
                        (r_strPassword.Equals("mas")))
  {
   strRoles = new string[1] ; strRoles[0] =
   "User" ;
  }
  return strRoles ;
  }
 }
}
```
Let's explore the code.

We start with the Init function. This function plugs in our handler for the AuthenticateRequest event into the Application object's event handlers list. This will cause the Application object to call this method whenever the AuthenticationRequest event is raised.

Once our HTTP module is initialized, its AuthenticateRequest method will be called for authenticating client requests. AuthenticateRequest method is the heart of the security/authentication mechanism. In that function:

Line 1 and Line 2 extract the HttpApplication and HttpContext objects. Line 3 through Line 7 checks whether any of the userid or password is not provided to us. If this is the case, error is displayed and the request processing is terminated.

Line 9 through Line 12 extract the user id and password from the HttpRequest object.

Line 14 calls a helper function, named AuthenticateAndGetRoles. This function basically performs the authentication and determines the user role. This has been hard-coded and only two users are allowed, but we can generalize this method and add code for interacting with some user database to retrieve user roles.

Advanced Web Tehnologies

Line 16 through Line 19 checks whether the user has any role assigned to it. If this is not the case that means the credentials passed to us could not be verified; therefore, these credentials are not valid. So, an error message is sent to the client and the request is completed.

Line 20 and Line 21 are very important because these lines actually inform the ASP.NET HTTP runtime about the identity of the logged-in user. Once these lines are successfully executed, our aspx pages will be able to access this information by using the User object.

Now let's see this authentication mechanism in action.
Currently we are only allowing the following users to log in to our system:

User id = Steve, Password = 15seconds, Role = Administrator

User id = Ajit, Password = mas, Role = User

Note that user id and password are case-sensitive.

First try logging-in without providing credentials. Go to http://localhost/webapp2/index.aspx and you should see the following message.

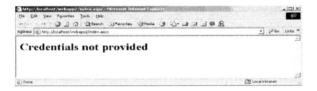

Now try logging-in with the user id "Steve" and password "15seconds". Go to http://localhost/webapp2/index.aspx?userid=Steve&password=15se conds and you should see the following welcome message.

Now try to log-in with the user id "Mansoor" and password "15seconds". Go to http://localhost/webapp2/index.aspx?userid=Mansoor&password=m as and you should see the following welcome page.

Now try to log-in with the wrong combination of user id and password. Go to

http://localhost/webapp2/index.aspx?userid=Mansoor&password=x yz and you should see the following error message.

This shows our security module in action. You can generalize this security module by using database-access code in the AuthenticateAndGetRoles method.

For all of this to work, we have to perform some changes in our web.config file. First of all, since we are using our own custom authentication, we don't need any other authentication mechanism. To specify this, change the <authentication> node in web.config file of webapp2 to look like this:

<authentication mode="None"/>

Similarly, don't allow anonymous users to our Web site. Add the following to web.config file:

```
<authorization>
 <deny users="?"/>
</authorization>
```

Users should at least have anonymous access to the file that they will use for providing credentials. Use the following configuration setting in the web.config file for specifying index.aspx as the only anonymously accessible file:

```
<location path="index.aspx">
 <system.web>
  <authorization>
   <allow users="*"/>
  </authorization>
 </system.web>
</location>
```

ASP.NET Page directives

Asp.Net web form page framework supports the following directives

@Page
@Master
@Control
@Register
@Reference
@PreviousPageType
@OutputCache
@Import
@Implements
@Assembly
@MasterType
@Page Directive

The @Page directive enables you to specify attributes and values for an Asp.Net Page to be used when the page is parsed and compiled. Every .aspx files should include this @Page directive to execute. There are many attributes belong to this directive. We shall discuss some of the important attributes here.

AspCompat: When set to True, this allows to the page to be executed on a single-threaded apartment. If you want to use a component developed in VB 6.0, you can set this value to True. But setting this attribute to true can cause your page's performance to degrade.

Language: This attribute tells the compiler about the language being used in the code-behind. Values can represent any .NET-supported language, including Visual Basic, C#, or JScript .NET.

AutoEventWireup: For every page there is an automatic way to bind the events to methods in the same .aspx file or in code behind.
The default value is true.

CodeFile: Specifies the code-behid file with which the page is associated.

Title: To set the page title other than what is specified in the master page.

Culture: Specifies the culture setting of the page. If you set to auto, enables the page to automatically detect the culture required for the page.

UICulture: Specifies the UI culture setting to use for the page. Supports any valid UI culture value.

ValidateRequest: Indicates whether request validation should occur. If set to true, request validation checks all input data against a hard-coded list of potentially dangerous values. If a match occurs, an HttpRequestValidationException Class is thrown. The default is true. This feature is enabled in the machine configuration file
(Machine.config). You can disable it in your application configuration file (Web.config) or on the page by setting this attribute to false.

Theme: To specify the theme for the page. This is a new feature available in Asp.Net 2.0.

SmartNavigation: Indicates the smart navigation feature of the page. When set to True, this returns the postback to current position of the page. The default value is false.

MasterPageFile: Specify the location of the MasterPage file to be used with the current Asp.Net page.

EnableViewState: Indicates whether view state is maintained across page requests. true if view state is maintained; otherwise, false. The default is true.

ErrorPage: Specifies a target URL for redirection if an unhandled page exception occurs.

Inherits: Specifies a code-behind class for the page to inherit.
This can be any class derived from the Page class.

There are also other attributes which are of seldom use such as Buffer, CodePage, ClassName, EnableSessionState,
Debug, Description, EnableTheming, EnableViewStateMac, TraceMode, WarningLevel, etc. Here is an example of how a @Page directive looks

```
<%@ Page Language="C#" AutoEventWireup="true"
CodeFile="Sample.aspx.cs" Inherits="Sample" Title="Sample
Page Title" %>
```

@Master Directive

The @Master directive is quite similar to the @Page directive. The @Master directive belongs to Master Pages that is .master files. The master page will be used in conjunction of any number of content pages. So the content pages can the inherits the attributes of the master page. Even though, both @Page and @Master page directives are similar, the @Master directive has only fewer attributes as follows

Language: This attribute tells the compiler about the language being used in the code-behind. Values can represent any .NET-supported language, including Visual Basic, C#, or JScript .NET.

AutoEventWireup: For every page there is an automatic way to bind the events to methods in the same master file or in code behind. The default value is True.

CodeFile: Specifies the code-behind file with which the MasterPage is associated

Title: Set the MasterPage Title.

MasterPageFile: Specifies the location of the MasterPage file to be used with the current MasterPage. This is called as Nested Master Page.

EnableViewState: Indicates whether view state is maintained across page requests. true if view state is maintained; otherwise, false. The default is true.

Inherits: Specifies a code-behind class for the page to inherit. This can be any class derived from the Page class.

Here is an example of how a @Master directive looks

```
<%@ Master Language="C#" AutoEventWireup="true"
CodeFile="WebMaster.master.cs" Inherits="WebMaster" %>
```

@Control Directive

The @Control directive is used when we build an Asp.Net user controls. The @Control directive helps us to define the properties to be inherited by the user control. These values are assigned to the user control as the page is parsed and c ompiled. The attributes of @Control directives are **Language:** This attribute tells the compiler about the language being used in the code-behind. Values can represent any .NET-supported language, including Visual Basic, C#, or JScript .NET.

AutoEventWireup: For every page there is an automatic way to bind the events to methods in the same .ascx file or in code behind.
The default value is true.

CodeFile: Specifies the code-behind file with which the user control is associated.

EnableViewState: Indicates whether view state is maintained across page requests. true if view state is maintained; otherwise, false. The default is true.

Inherits: Specifies a code-behind class for the page to inherit.
This can be any class derived from the Page class.

Debug: Indicates whether the page should be compiled with debug symbols.

Src: Points to the source file of the class used for the code behind of the user control.

The other attributes which are very rarely used is
ClassName, CompilerOptions, ComplieWith, Description, EnableTheming, Explicit, LinePragmas, Strict and WarningLevel.

Here is an example of how a @Control directive looks

```
<%@ Control Language="C#" AutoEventWireup="true"
CodeFile="MyControl.ascx.cs" Inherits=" MyControl " %>
```

@Register Directive

The @Register directive associates aliases with namespaces and class names for notation in custom server control syntax. When you drag and drop a user control onto your .aspx pages, the Visual Studio 2005 automatically creates an @Register directive at the top of the page. This register the user control on the page so that the control can be accessed on the .aspx page by a specific name.

The main attribues of @Register directive are

Assembly: The assembly you are associating with the TagPrefix.

Namespace: The namspace to relate with TagPrefix.

Src: The location of the user control.

TagName: The alias to relate to the class name.

TagPrefix: The alias to relate to the namespace.

Here is an example of how a @Register directive looks

```
<%@ Register Src="Yourusercontrol.ascx" TagName="
Yourusercontrol " TagPrefix="uc1"
Src="~\usercontrol\usercontrol1.ascx" %>
```

@Reference Directive

The @Reference directive declares that another asp.net page or user control should be complied along with the current page or user control. The 2 attributes for @Reference directive are

Control: User control that ASP.NET should dynamically compile and link to the current page at run time.

Page: The Web Forms page that ASP.NET should dynamically compile and link to the current page at run time.

VirutalPath: Specifies the location of the page or user control from which the active page will be referenced.

Here is an example of how a @Reference directive looks

```
<%@ Reference VirutalPath="YourReferencePage.ascx" %>
```

@PreviousPageType Directive

The @PreviousPageType is a new directive makes excellence in asp.net 2.0 pages. The concept of cross-page posting between Asp.Net pages is achieved by this directive. This directive is used to specify the page from which the cross-page posting initiates. This simple directive contains only two attiributes

TagName: Sets the name of the derived class from which the postback will occur.

VirutalPath: sets the location of the posting page from which the postback will occur.

Here is an example of @PreviousPageType directive

```
<%@ PreviousPageType
VirtualPath="~/YourPreviousPageName.aspx" %>
```

@OutputCache Directive

The @OutputCache directive controls the output caching policies of the Asp.Net page or user control. You can even cache programatically through code by using Visual Basic .NET or Visual C# .NET. The very important attributes for the @OutputCache directive are as follows

Duration: The duration of time in seconds that the page or user control is cached.

Location: To specify the location to store the output cache. To store the output cache on the browser client where the request originated set the value as 'Client'. To store the output cache on any HTTP 1.1 cache-capable devices including the proxy servers and the client that made request, specify the Location as Downstream. To store the output cache on the Web server, mention the location as Server.

VaryByParam: List of strings used to vary the output cache, separated with semi-colon.

VaryByControl: List of strings used to vary the output cache of a user Control, separated with semi-colon.

VaryByCustom: String of values, specifies the custom output caching requirements.

VaryByHeader: List of HTTP headers used to vary the output cache, separated with semi-colon.

The other attribues which is rarely used are CacheProfile, DiskCacheable, NoStore, SqlDependency, etc.

```
<%@ OutputCache Duration="60"
Location="Server" VaryByParam="None" %>
```

To turn off the output cache for an ASP.NET Web page at the client location and at the proxy location, set the Location attribute value to none, and then set the VaryByParam value to none in the @ OutputCache directive. Use the following code samples to turn off client and proxy caching.

```
<%@ OutputCache Location="None" VaryByParam="None" %>
```

Advanced Web Tehnologies

@Import Directive

The @Import directive allows you to specify any namespaces to the imported to the Asp.Net pages or user controls. By importing, all the classes and interfaces of the namespace are made available to the page or user control. The example of the @Import directive

```
<%@ Import namespace="System.Data" %>
<%@ Import namespace="System.Data.SqlClient" %>
```

@Implements Directive

The @Implements directive gets the Asp.Net page to implement a specified .NET framework interface. The only single attribute is Interface, helps to specify the .NET Framework interface. When the Asp.Net page or user control implements an interface, it has direct access to all its events, methods and properties.

```
<%@ Implements Interface="System.Web.UI.IValidator" %>
```

@Assembly Directive

The @Assembly directive is used to make your ASP.NET page aware of external components. This directive supports two attributes:
a. Name: Enables you specify the name of an assembly you want to attach to the page. Here you should mention the filename without the extension.
b. Src: represents the name of a source code file

```
<%@ Assembly Name="YourAssemblyName" %>
```

@MasterType Directive

To access members of a specific master page from a content page, you can create a strongly typed reference to the master page by creating a @MasterType directive. This directive supports of two attributes such as TypeName and VirtualPath.

TypeName: Sets the name of the derived class from which to get strongly typed references or members.

VirtualPath: Sets the location of the master page from which the strongly typed references and members will be retrieved.

If you have public properties defined in a Master Page that you'd like to access in a strongly-typed manner you can add the MasterType directive into a page as shown next

Questions:

2.1: What is the use of @ Register directives?

2.2: What are directives ? Which are the directives used in ASP ?

2.3: What is Page Directive?

Page Event and Page Life Cycle

General Page Life-cycle Stages
Stage
Description

Page request
The page request occurs before the page life cycle begins. When the page is requested by a user, ASP.NET determines whether the page needs to be parsed and compiled or whether a cached version of the page can be sent in response without running the page.

Start
In the start step, page properties such as Request and Response are set. At this stage, the page also determines whether the request is a postback or a new request and sets the IsPostBack property. Additionally, during the start step, the page's UICulture property is set.

Page initialization
During page initialization, controls on the page are available and each control's UniqueID property is set. Any themes are also applied to the page. If the current request is a postback, the postback data has not yet been loaded and control property values have not been restored to the values from view state.

Load
During load, if the current request is a postback, control properties are loaded with information recovered from view state and control state.

Validation
During validation, the Validate method of all validator controls is called, which sets the IsValid property of individual validator controls and of the page.

Postback event handling
If the request is a postback, any event handlers are called.

Rendering
Before rendering, view state is saved for the page and all controls. During the rendering phase, the page calls the Render method for each control, providing a text writer that writes its output to the OutputStream of the page's Response property.

Unload
Unload is called after the page has been fully rendered, sent to the client, and is ready to be discarded. At this point, page properties such as Response and Request are unloaded and any cleanup is performed.

Data Binding Events for Data-Bound Controls
Control Event

Typical Use

DataBinding

This event is raised by data-bound controls before the PreRender event of the containing control (or of the Page object) and marks the beginning of binding the control to the data.

RowCreated	(GridView)
ItemCreated	(DataList,
DetailsView,	SiteMapPath,
DataGrid,	FormView,
Repeater)	

Use this event to manipulate content that is not dependent on data binding. For example, at run time, you might programmatically add formatting to a header or footer row in a GridView control.

RowDataBound	(GridView)
ItemDataBound	(DataList,
SiteMapPath,	DataGrid,
Repeater)	

When this event occurs, data is available in the row or item, so you can format data or set the FilterExpression property on child data source controls for displaying related data within the row or item.

DataBound

This event marks the end of data-binding operations in a data-bound control. In a GridView control, data binding is complete for all rows and any child controls. Use this event to format data bound content or to initiate data binding in other controls that depend on values from the current control's content.

Common Life-cycle Events

Page Event
Typical Use
PreInit

Use this event for the following:

Check the IsPostBack property to determine whether this is the first time the page is being processed.

Create or re-create dynamic controls.
Set a master page dynamically.
Set the Theme property dynamically.
Read or set profile property values.

Note: If the request is a postback, the values of the controls have not yet been restored from view state. If you set a control property at this stage, its value might be overwritten in the next event.

Init

Raised after all controls have been initialized and any skin settings have been applied. Use this event to read or initialize control properties.

InitComplete

Raised by the Page object. Use this event for processing tasks that require all initialization be complete.

PreLoad

Use this event if you need to perform processing on your page or control before the Load event. After the Page raises this event, it loads view state for itself and all controls, and then processes any postback data included with the Request instance.

Load

The Page calls the OnLoad event method on the Page, then recursively does the same for each child control, which does the same for each of its child controls until the page and all controls are loaded.

Control events

Use these events to handle specific control events, such as a Button control's Click event or a TextBox control's TextChanged event. In a postback request, if the page contains validator controls, check the IsValid property of the Page and of individual validation controls before performing any processing.

LoadComplete

Use this event for tasks that require that all other controls on the page be loaded.

PreRender

Before this event occurs:

The Page object calls EnsureChildControls for each control and for the page.

Each data bound control whose DataSourceID property is set calls its DataBind method.

The PreRender event occurs for each control on the page. Use the event to make final changes to the contents of the page or its controls.

SaveStateCompleteBefore this event occurs, ViewState has been saved for the page and for all controls. Any changes to the page or controls at this point will be ignored. Use this event perform tasks that require view state to be saved, but that do not make any changes to controls.

Render

This is not an event; instead, at this stage of processing, the Page object calls this method on each control. All ASP.NET Web server controls have a Render method that writes out the control's markup that is sent to the browser. If you create a custom control, you typically override this method to output the control's markup. However, if your custom control incorporates only standard ASP.NET Web server controls and no custom markup, you do not need to override the Render method. A user control (an .ascx file) automatically incorporates rendering, so you do not need to explicitly render the control in code.

Unload

This event occurs for each control and then for the page. In controls, use this event to do final cleanup for specific controls, such as closing control-specific database connections. For the page itself, use this event to do final cleanup work, such as closing open files and database connections, or finishing up logging or other request-specific tasks. Note: During the unload stage, the page and its controls have been rendered, so you cannot make further changes to the response stream. If you attempt to call a method such as the Response.Write method, the page will throw an exception.

List the various stages of Page-Load lifecycle.?

What's the sequence in which ASP.NET events are processed?

What is event bubbling ?

PostBack and CrossPage Posting
PostBack

Programming model in old ASP for using POST method in form is to post the values of a Form to a second page. The second asp page will receive the data and process it for doing any validation or processing on the server side. With ASP .Net, the whole model has changed. Each of the asp .net pages will be a separate entity with ability to process itsown posted data. That is, the values of the Form are posted to the same page and the very same page can process the data. This model is called post back.

Each Asp .net page when loaded goes through a regular creation and destruction cycle like Initialization, Page load etc., in the beginning and unload while closing it. This Postback is a read only property with each Asp .Net Page (System.Web.UI.Page) class. This is false when the first time the page is loaded and is true when the page is submitted and processed. This enables users to write the code depending on if the PostBack is true or false (with the use of the function Page.IsPostBack()).

Implementation of ASP.Net Post back on the Client side:

Post back is implemented with the use javascript in the client side. The HTML page generated for each .aspx page will have the action property of the form tag set to the same page. This makes the page to be posted on to itself. If we check the entry on the HTML file, it will look something like this.

```
<form name="_ctl1" method="post"
action="pagename.aspx?getparameter1=134" language="javascript"
onsubmit="if (!ValidatorOnSubmit()) return false;" id="_ctl1" >
```

Also, all the validation code that is written (Required Field Validation, Regular Expression validation etc.,) will all be processed at the client side using the .js(javascript) file present in the webserver_wwwroot/aspnet_client folder.

With this new ASP .Net model, even if the user wants to post the data to a different .aspx page, the web server will check for the runat='server' tag in the form tag and post the web form to the same .aspx page. A simple declaration as

151

in the following code snippet will be enough to create such a web form.

```
<form id="form1" runat="server" >
<!-- place the controls inside --> </form>
```

Cross Page posting or cross page postback is used to submit a form on one page (say default.aspx) and retrieve values of controls of this page on another page (say Default2.aspx)

```
<%@ Page Language="C#" AutoEventWireup="true"
CodeFile="Default.aspx.cs" Inherits="_Default" %>

<!DOCTYPE html PUBLIC "-//W3C//DTD XHTML 1.0
Transitional//EN" "http://www.w3.org/TR/xhtml1/DTD/xhtml1-transitional.dtd">

<html xmlns="http://www.w3.org/1999/xhtml" >
<head runat="server">
<title>Untitled Page</title>
</head>
<body>
<form id="form1" runat="server">
<div>
First Name:
<asp:TextBox ID="txtFirstName" runat="server">
</asp:TextBox><br /><br /> Last Name:
<asp:TextBox ID="txtLastName" runat="server"> </asp:TextBox><br
/><br /><br />

<asp:Button ID="btnSubmit" runat="server"
        OnClick="btnSubmit_Click" PostBackUrl="~/Default2.aspx"
        Text="Submit to Second Page" /><br />
</div>
</form>
</body>
</html>
```

Don't forget to set PostBackUrl Property of Button
PostBackUrl="~/Default2.aspx"

Now to retrieve values of textBoxes on Default2.aspx page, write below mentioned code in Page_Load event of second page (Default2.aspx)

C# code behind

```
protected void Page_Load(object sender, EventArgs e)
{
//Check whether previous page is cross page post back or not
if (PreviousPage != null &&
PreviousPage.IsCrossPagePostBack)
{
TextBox txtPbFirstName =
(TextBox)PreviousPage.FindControl("txtFirstName");
TextBox txtPbLastName =
(TextBox)PreviousPage.FindControl("txtLastName");
Label1.Text = "Welcome " + txtPbFirstName.Text + " " + txtPbLastName.Text;
.}
else
{
Response.Redirect("Default.aspx");
}
}
```

VB.NET Code behind

```
Protected Sub Page_Load(ByVal sender As Object, ByVa l e As EventArgs)
'Check whether previous page is cross page post back or not
If PreviousPage IsNot Nothing AndAlsoPreviousPage.IsCrossPagePostBack
Then
Dim txtPbFirstName As TextBox
=DirectCast(PreviousPage.FindControl("txtFirstName"),
TextBox)
Dim txtPbLastName As TextBox
=DirectCast(PreviousPage.FindControl("txtLastName"), TextBox)
Label1.Text = ("Welcome " & txtPbFirstName.Text & " ") + txtPbLastName.Text
Else
Response.Redirect("Default.aspx")
End If
End Sub
```

If you are using masterpages then you need to write code to FindControl as mentioned below

```
ContentPlaceHolder exampleHolder
=(ContentPlaceHolder)Page.PreviousPage.Form.FindContro l ("Content1"));
TextBox txtExample = exampleHolder.FindControl("txtFirstName");
```

Questions:

What is Postback?
What is CrossPage Posting?
What' is the sequence in which ASP.NET events are processed?
In which event are the controls fully loaded?

ASP.NET Application Compilation Models
ASP.NET Compilation

This information is not vital to your success as an ASP.NET developer, but having an understanding of the architecture of your development environment always makes you a better developer.

ASP.NET is nothing like the legacy ASP with which many developers are familiar. You develop ASP pages by using VBScript or JScript, and they are interpreted, meaning that they are executed just as they are written, directly from the page. ASP.NET is entirely different in that ASP.NET pages are compiled before they are executed.

When you write ASP.NET code, you do so in human-readable text. Before ASP.NET can run your code, it has to convert it into something that the computer can understand and execute. The process of converting code from what a programmer types into what a computer can actually execute is called *compilation*.

Exactly how compilation takes place in ASP.NET depends on the compilation model that you use. Several different compilation models are available to you in ASP.NET 4.0.

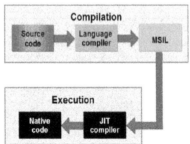

The Web Application Compilation Model

The web application compilation model is the same model provided in ASP.NET 1.0 and 1.1. When you use this model, you use the Build menu in Visual Web Developer to compile your application into a single DLL file that is copied to a bin folder in the root of your application. When the first request comes into your application, the DLL from the bin folder is copied to the Temporary ASP.NET Files folder, where it is then recompiled into code that the operating system can execute in a process known as *just-in-time (JIT)* compilation. The JIT compilation causes a delay of several seconds on the first request of the application.

NOTE
The web application model is available only in Visual Studio 2008. Visual Web Developer 2008 does not enable you to create ASP.NET applications using the web application model.

NOTE
The Temporary ASP.NET Files folder is located at Windows\Microsoft.NET\Framework\v2.0.50727\Temporary ASP.NET Files by default.

To create a new ASP.NET web application using the web application compilation model, select File, New Project, and then choose the ASP.NET Web Application template.

Choose the New Project option on the File menu to create a new ASP.NET application that uses the web application compilation model.

ASP.NET Server Controls

ASP.NET - Server Controls
ASP.NET has solved the "spaghetti-code" problem described above with server controls.
Server controls are tags that are understood by the server.
There are three kinds of server controls:
HTML Server Controls - Traditional HTML tags
Web Server Controls - New ASP.NET tags
Validation Server Controls - For input validation
ASP.NET - HTML Server Controls
HTML server controls are HTML tags understood by the server.

HTML elements in ASP.NET files are, by default, treated as text. To make these elements programmable, add a runat="server" attribute to the HTML element. This attribute indicates that the element should be treated as a server control. The id attribute is added to identify the server control. The id reference can be used to manipulate the server control at run time.

Note: All HTML server controls must be within a <form> tag with the runat="server" attribute. The runat="server" attribute indicates that the form should be processed on the server. It also indicates that the enclosed controls can be accessed by server scripts.

In the following example we declare an HtmlAnchor server control in an .aspx file. Then we manipulate the HRef attribute of the HtmlAnchor control in an event handler (an event handler is a subroutine that executes code for a given event). The Page_Load event is one of many events that
ASP.NET understands:

```
<script runat="server">
Sub                               Page_Load
link1.HRef="http://www.w3schools.com" End Sub
</script>
<html>
<body>
<form runat="server">
<a id="link1" runat="server">Visit W3Schools!</a>
</form>
</body>
</html>
```

ASP.NET - Web Server Controls
Web server controls are special ASP.NET tags understood by the server.
Like HTML server controls, Web server controls are also created on the server and they require a runat="server" attribute to work. However, Web server controls do not necessarily map to any existing HTML elements and they may represent more complex elements.
The syntax for creating a Web server control is:
<asp:control_name id="some_id" runat="server" />

In the following example we declare a Button server control in an .aspx file. Then we create an event handler for the Click event which changes the text on the button:

```
<script runat="server">
```

```
Sub    submit(Source    As    Object,    e    As    EventArgs)
button1.Text="You clicked me!"
End Sub
</script>
<html>
<body>
<form runat="server">
<asp:Button       id="button1"       Text="Click       me!"
runat="server" OnClick="submit"/>
</form>
</body>
</html>
```

ASP.NET - Validation Server Controls

Validation server controls are used to validate user-input. If the user-input does not pass validation, it will display an error message to the user.

Each validation control performs a specific type of validation (like validating against a specific value or a range of values).

By default, page validation is performed when a Button,
ImageButton, or LinkButton control is clicked. You can prevent validation when a button control is clicked by setting the
CausesValidation property to false.

The syntax for creating a Validation server control is:

```
<asp:control_name id="some_id" runat="server" />
```
In the following example we declare one TextBox control, one Button control, and one RangeValidator control in an .aspx file. If validation fails, the text "The value must be from 1 to 100!" will be displayed in the RangeValidator control:

```
<html>
<body>
<form runat="server">
<p>Enter a number from 1 to 100: <asp:TextBox
id="tbox1" runat="server" />
<br /><br />
<asp:Button Text="Submit" runat="server" />
</p>
<p>
<asp:RangeValidator
ControlToValidate="tbox1"
MinimumValue="1"
MaximumValue="100"
Type="Integer"
```

```
            Text="The value must be from 1 to 100!"
            runat="server" />
            </p>
            </form>
            </body>
            </html>
```

Questions:

How to set view state for server control? Enableviewstate property?

HTML Controls
HtmlControls In ASP.NET

System.Web.UI.HtmlControls namespace is often ignored by ASP.NET developers. There is an opinion that **System.Web.UI.WebControls** classes are more natural to ASP.NET web application and I agree with that. However, HtmlControls namespace is still standard part of .Net Framework just like WebControls. You can drag it from toolbox and easily drop it to your web form. HtmlControls have its advantages in some scenarios and you **should know both namespaces** so you can decide which class to use in your specific case.

HtmlControls are just programmable HTML tags. By default these tags are literal text and you can't reference them with server side code. To "see" any HTML tag with your ASP.NET server side code you need to add runat="server" and some value to ID parameter. For example, to work with <textarea> HTML tag with server side code, you can use HTML code like this:

```
<textarea runat="server" id="TextArea1" cols="20" rows="2"></textarea>
```

So, nothing hard here, we just set value of id property and add runat="server" part. After this, we can manipulate with this tag with
C# or VB.NET server side code, like this:

```
[ C# ]
protected void Page_Load(object sender, EventArgs e)
{
  // set new size of textarea
  TextArea1.Cols = 15;
}
```

```
[ VB.NET ]
Protected Sub Page_Load(ByVal sender As Object, ByVal e As
System.EventArgs) Handles Me.Load ' set new size
  of textarea TextArea1.Cols = 15
End Sub
```

HtmlControls are much less abstract than WebControls. With HtmlControls you work directly with HTML output. WebControls are not always rendered on the same way. For example TextBox control is rendered as <input type="text" /> tag if value of its TextMode property is SingleLine but TextBox will render as
<textarea > if TextMode=MultiLine.

How to apply styles to HtmlControls

HtmlControls have not styles property so you can't set style directly.
To apply styles to HtmlControls you need to use Attributes property, with code like this:

[C#]
TextArea1.Attributes["Style"] = "FONT-FAMILY: 'Arial'; COLOR: blue; BACKGROUND-COLOR: yellow";

[VB.NET]
TextArea1.Attributes("Style") = "FONT-FAMILY: 'Arial'; COLOR: blue; BACKGROUND-COLOR: yellow"217

Questions:

1. What are HTML server controls and Web controls ?

Validation Controls

With ASP.NET, there are six(6) controls included. They are:
The RequiredFieldValidation Control
The CompareValidator Control
The RangeValidator Control
The RegularExpressionValidator Control
The CustomValidator Control

Validator Control Basics

All of the validation controls inherit from the base class BaseValidator so they all have a series of properties and methods that are common to all validation controls. They are:

ControlToValidate - This value is which control the validator is applied to.
ErrorMessage - This is the error message that will be displayed in the validation summary.
IsValid - Boolean value for whether or not the control is valid.
Validate - Method to validate the input control and update the IsValid property.

Display - This controls how the error message is shown. Here are the possible options:
> None (The validation message is never displayed.)
> Static (Space for the validation message is allocated in the page layout.)
> Dynamic (Space for the validation message is dynamically added to the page if validation fails.)

The RequiredFieldValidation Control

The first control we have is the RequiredFieldValidation Control. As it's obvious, it make sure that a user inputs a value. Here is how it's used:

```
Required field: <asp:textbox id="textbox1" runat="server"/>

<asp:RequiredFieldValidator id="valRequired" runat="server"
ControlToValidate="textbox1"

    ErrorMessage="* You must enter a value into textbox1"
Display="dynamic">*

</asp:RequiredFieldValidator>
```

In this example, we have a textbox which will not be valid until the user types something in. Inside the validator tag, we have a single *. The text in the innerhtml will be shown in the controltovalidate if the control is not valid. It should be noted that the *ErrorMessage* attribute is not what is shown. The ErrorMessage tag is shown in the Validation Summary (see below).

The CompareValidator Control

Next we look at the CompareValidator Control. Usage of this CompareValidator is for confirming new passwords, checking if a departure date is before the arrival date, etc. We'll start of with a sample:

```
Textbox 1: <asp:textbox id="textbox1" runat="server"/><br />
Textbox 2: <asp:textbox id="textbox2" runat="server"/><br />
<asp:CompareValidator id="valCompare" runat="server"
    ControlToValidate="textbox1"
    ControlToCompare="textbox2"
    Operator="Equals"
    ErrorMessage="* You must enter the same values into textbox 1
    and textbox 2"
    Display="dynamic">*
</asp:CompareValidator>
```

Advanced Web Tehnologies

Here we have a sample where the two textboxes must be equal. The tags that are unique to this control is the *ControlToCompare* attribute which is the control that will be compared. The two controls are compared with the type of comparison specified in the *Operator* attribute. The *Operator* attribute can contain Equal, GreterThan, LessThanOrEqual, etc.

Another usage of the ComapareValidator is to have a control compare to a value.

For example:

```
Field: <asp:textbox id="textbox1" runat="server"/>
       <asp:CompareValidator id="valRequired" runat="server"
       ControlToValidate="textbox1"
         ValueToCompare="50"
         Type="Integer"
         Operator="GreaterThan"
         ErrorMessage="* You must enter the a number greater than 50"
       Display="dynamic">*
       </asp:CompareValidator>
```

The data type can be one of: Currency, Double, Date, Integer or String. String being the default data type.

The RangeValidator Control

Range validator control is another validator control which checks to see if a control value is within a valid range. The attributes that are necessary to this control are: *MaximumValue, MinimumValue*, and *Type*.

Sample:

```
       Enter a date from 1998:
       <asp:textbox id="textbox1" runat="server"/>
       <asp:RangeValidator id="valRange" runat="server"
         ControlToValidate="textbox1"
         MaximumValue="12/31/1998"
         MinimumValue="1/1/1998"

         Type="Date"
         ErrorMessage="* The date must be between 1/1/1998 and
       12/13/1998" Display="static">*</asp:RangeValidator>
```

Advanced Web Tehnologies

The RegularExpressionValidator Control

The regular expression validator is one of the more powerful features of ASP.NET. Everyone loves regular expressions.
Especially when you write those really big nasty ones... and then a few days later, look at it and say to yourself. What does this do? Again, the simple usage is:

```
E-mail: <asp:textbox id="textbox1" runat="server"/>
    <asp:RegularExpressionValidator id="valRegEx" runat="server"
    ControlToValidate="textbox1"
    ValidationExpression=".*@.*\..*"
    ErrorMessage="* Your entry is not a valid e-mail address."
    display="dynamic">*
    </asp:RegularExpressionValidator>
```

The CustomValidator Control

The final control we have included in ASP.NET is one that adds great flexibility to our validation abilities. We have a custom validator where we get to write out own functions and pass the control value to this function.

```
Field: <asp:textbox id="textbox1" runat="server">
<asp:CustomValidator id="valCustom" runat="server"
    ControlToValidate="textbox1"
    ClientValidationFunction="ClientValidate"
    OnServerValidate="ServerValidate"
    ErrorMessage="*This box is not valid"

    display="dynamic">*

</asp:CustomValidator>
```

We notice that there are two new attributes *ClientValidationFunction* and *OnServerValidate*. These are the tell the validation control which functions to pass the controltovalidate value to. ClientValidationFunction is usually a javascript function included in the html to the user. OnServerValidate is the function that is server-side to check for validation if client does not support client -side validation.

```
Client Validation function:
    <script language="Javascript">
    <!--
      /* ... Code goes here ... */
    -->
    </script>
```

```
Server Validation function:
    Sub   ServerValidate  (objSource   As   Object,   objArgs   As
    ServerValidateEventsArgs)
```

```
    ' Code goes here
    End Sub
```

Validation Summary

ASP.NET has provided an additional control that complements the validator controls. This is the validation summary control which is used like:

```
<asp:ValidationSummary id="valSummary" runat="server"
    HeaderText="Errors:" ShowSummary="true" DisplayMode="List" />
```

The validation summary control will collect all the error messages of all the non-valid controls and put them in a tidy list.
The list can be either shown on the web page (as shown in the example above) or with a popup box (by specifying
ShowMessageBox="True")

Questions:

How many types of validation controls are provided by ASP.NET?

Which two properties on validation control?

What type of data validation events are commonly seen in the client-side form validation?

Which control is used to make sure the values in two different controls are matched?

How do you validate the controls in ASP.NET page?

Name two properties common in every validation control.

Building Databases

Create a Database Connection

We are going to use the Northwind database in our examples. First, import the "System.Data.OleDb" namespace. We need this namespace to work with Microsoft Access and other OLE DB database providers. We will create the connection to the database in the Page_Load subroutine. We create a dbconn variable as a new OleDbConnection class with a connection string which identifies the OLE DB provider and the location of the database. Then we open the database connection

```
<%@ Import Namespace="System.Data.OleDb" %>
<script runat="server">
sub Page_Load
dim dbconn dbconn=New
OleDbConnection("Provider=Microsoft.Jet.OLEDB.4.0; data source=" &
server.mappath("northwind.mdb")) dbconn.Open()
```

```
end sub
</script>
```

Create a Database Command

To specify the records to retrieve from the database, we will create a dbcomm variable as a new OleDbCommand class. The OleDbCommand class is for issuing SQL queries against database tables:

```
<%@ Import Namespace="System.Data.OleDb" %>
<script runat="server">
sub Page_Load
dim dbconn,sql,dbcomm dbconn=New
OleDbConnection("Provider=Microsoft.Jet.OLEDB.4.0; data source=" &
server.mappath("northwind.mdb")) dbconn.Open()
sql="SELECT * FROM customers" dbcomm=New
OleDbCommand(sql,dbconn)
end sub
</script>
```

Create a DataReader

The OleDbDataReader class is used to read a stream of records from a data source. A DataReader is created by calling the ExecuteReader method of the OleDbCommand object:.

```
<%@ Import Namespace="System.Data.OleDb" %>
<script runat="server">
sub Page_Load
dim dbconn,sql,dbcomm,dbread
dbconn=New
OleDbConnection("Provider=Microsoft.Jet.OLEDB.4.0; data source=" &
server.mappath("northwind.mdb")) dbconn.Open()
sql="SELECT * FROM customers" dbcomm=New
OleDbCommand(sql,dbconn)
dbread=dbcomm.ExecuteReader()
end sub
</script>
```

Bind to a Repeater Control

Then we bind the DataReader to a Repeater control:

```
<%@ Import Namespace="System.Data.OleDb" %>
<script runat="server">
sub Page_Load
```

```
dim dbconn,sql,dbcomm,dbread
dbconn=New
OleDbConnection("Provider=Microsoft.Jet.OLEDB.4.0; data source=" &
server.mappath("northwind.mdb")) dbconn.Open()
sql="SELECT * FROM customers" dbcomm=New
OleDbCommand(sql,dbconn) dbread=dbcomm.ExecuteReader()
customers.DataSource=dbread customers.DataBind()
dbread.Close()
dbconn.Close()
end sub
</script>
<html>
<body>
<form runat="server">
<asp:Repeater id="customers" runat="server">
<HeaderTemplate>
<table border="1" width="100%"> <tr>
<th>Companyname</th>
<th>Contactname</th>
<th>Address</th>
<th>City</th>
</tr>
</HeaderTemplate>
<ItemTemplate>
<tr>
<td><%#Container.DataItem("companyname")%></td>
<td><%#Container.DataItem("contactname")%></td>
<td><%#Container.DataItem("address")%></td>
<td><%#Container.DataItem("city")%></td>
</tr>
</ItemTemplate>
<FooterTemplate>
</table>
</FooterTemplate>
</asp:Repeater>
</form>
</body>
</html>
```

Close the Database Connection

Always close both the DataReader and database connection after access to the
database is no longer required:
```
dbread.Close()
dbconn.Close()
```

165

Exercise:

What is ADO .NET and what is difference between ADO and ADO.NET?

Give the comparision between C# and ASP.NET?

List an explain the steps for loading the simple ASP.NET web application?

What is the role of web.config file?

What is container class?

Write the steps for implementing the Asp.NET application with Database.

## 8

XML

XML

What is XML?

XML stands for EXtensible Markup Language.
XML is a markup language much like HTML.
XML was designed to carry data, not to display data.
XML tags are not predefined. You must define your own tags.
XML is designed to be self-descriptive.
XML is a W3C Recommendation.

The Difference Between XML and HTML:

XML is not a replacement for HTML.
XML and HTML were designed with different goals:
XML was designed to transport and store data, with focus on what data is.
HTML was designed to display data, with focus on how data looks.
HTML is about displaying information, while XML is about carrying information.

With XML You Invent Your Own Tags:

The tags are "invented" by the author of the XML document.
That is because the XML language has no predefined tags.
The tags used in HTML are predefined. HTML documents can only use tags defined in the HTML standard (like <p>, <h1>, etc.).
XML allows the author to define his/her own tags and his/her own document structure.

XML is Not a Replacement for HTML:

XML is a complement to HTML.
It is important to understand that XML is not a replacement for HTML. In most web applications, XML is used to transport data, while HTML is used to format and display the data.

XML is a software- and hardware-independent tool for carrying information.

XML is a W3C Recommendation

XML became a W3C Recommendation 10. February 1998.

XML is Everywhere

XML is now as important for the Web as HTML was to the foundation of the Web.

XML is the most common tool for data transmissions between all sorts of applications.

XML is used in many aspects of web development, often to simplify data storage and sharing.

XML Separates Data from HTML

If you need to display dynamic data in your HTML document, it will take a lot of work to edit the HTML each time the data changes.

With XML, data can be stored in separate XML files. This way you can concentrate on using HTML for layout and display, and be sure that changes in the underlying data will not require any changes to the HTML.

With a few lines of JavaScript code, you can read an external XML file and update the data content of your web page.

XML Simplifies Data Sharing

In the real world, computer systems and databases contain data in incompatible formats.

XML data is stored in plain text format. This provides a software- and hardware-independent way of storing data.

This makes it much easier to create data that can be shared by different applications.

XML Simplifies Data Transport

One of the most time-consuming challenges for developers is to exchange data between incompatible systems over the Internet.

Exchanging data as XML greatly reduces this complexity, since the data can be read by different incompatible applications.

Advanced Web Tehnologies

XML Simplifies Platform Changes

Upgrading to new systems (hardware or software platforms), is always time consuming. Large amounts of data must be converted and incompatible data is often lost.

XML data is stored in text format. This makes it easier to expand or upgrade to new operating systems, new applications, or new browsers, without losing data.

XML Makes Your Data More Available

Different applications can access your data, not only in HTML pages, but also from XML data sources.

With XML, your data can be available to all kinds of "reading machines" (Handheld computers, voice machines, news feeds, etc), and make it more available for blind people, or people with other disabilities.

XML is Used to Create New Internet Languages

A lot of new Internet languages are created with XML.
Here are some examples:
    XHTML
    WSDL (Web Services Description Language) for describing available web services
    WAP and WML as markup languages for handheld devices
    RSS languages for news feeds
    RDF and OWL for describing resources and ontology
    SMIL for describing multimedia for the web

XML Documents Form a Tree Structure

XML documents must contain a root element. This element is "the parent" of all other elements.

The elements in an XML document form a document tree.
The tree starts at the root and branches to the lowest level of the tree.

All elements can have sub elements (child elements):

```
<root>
 <child>
  <subchild>.....</subchild>
 </child>
</root>
```

The terms parent, child, and sibling are used to describe the relationships between elements. Parent elements have children. Children on the same level are called siblings (brothers or sisters).

Advanced Web Tehnologies

All elements can have text content and attributes (just like in HTML).

SYNTAX

The syntax rules of XML are very simple and logical. The rules are easy to learn, and easy to use.

All XML Elements Must Have a Closing Tag

In HTML, elements do not have to have a closing tag:

```
<p>This is a paragraph
<p>This is another paragraph
```

In XML, it is illegal to omit the closing tag. All elements must have a closing tag:
```
<p>This is a paragraph</p>
<p>This is another paragraph</p>
```

XML Tags are Case Sensitive

XML tags are case sensitive. The tag <Letter> is different from the tag <letter>.

Opening and closing tags must be written with the same case:

```
<Message>This is incorrect</message>
<message>This is correct</message>
```

XML Elements Must be Properly Nested:

In HTML, you might see improperly nested elements:
```
<b><i>This text is bold and italic</b></i>
```
In XML, all elements must be properly nested within each other:
```
<b><i>This text is bold and italic</i></b>
```

In the example above, "Properly nested" simply means that since the <i> element is opened inside the <b> element, it must be closed inside the <b> element.

XML Documents Must Have a Root Element:

XML documents must contain one element that is the parent of all other elements. This element is called the root element.
```
<root>
 <child>
  <subchild>.....</subchild>
 </child>
</root>
```

XML Attribute Values Must be Quoted

XML elements can have attributes in name/value pairs just like in
HTML.
In XML, the attribute values must always be quoted.
Study the two XML documents below. The first one is incorrect, the second is
correct:

```
<note date=12/11/2007>
<to>Tove</to>
  <from>Jani</from>
</note>
```

```
<note date="12/11/2007">
<to>Tove</to>
  <from>Jani</from>
</note>
```

The error in the first document is that the date attribute in the note element is not
quoted.

Entity References

Some characters have a special meaning in XML.
If you place a character like "<" inside an XML element, it will generate an error
because the parser interprets it as the start of a new element.
This will generate an XML error:

```
message>if salary < 1000 then</message>
```

To avoid this error, replace the "<" character with an **entity reference:**

```
<message>if salary &lt; 1000 then</message>
```

There are 5 predefined entity references in XML:

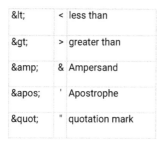

<	<	less than
>	>	greater than
&	&	Ampersand
'	'	Apostrophe
"	"	quotation mark

Advanced Web Tehnologies

Comments in XML:

The syntax for writing comments in XML is similar to that of HTML.
<!-- This is a comment -->

White-space is Preserved in XML

HTML truncates multiple white-space characters to one single white-space:

HTML:	Hello Tove
Output:	Hello Tove

With XML, the white-space in a document is not truncated.

XML Stores New Line as LF

In Windows applications, a new line is normally stored as a pair of characters: carriage return (CR) and line feed (LF). In Unix applications, a new line is normally stored as a LF character. Macintosh applications also use an LF to store a new line. XML stores a new line as LF.

DTDs and XML Schema

DTD

A Document Type Definition (DTD) defines the legal building blocks of an XML document. It defines the document structure with a list of legal elements and attributes.

A DTD can be declared inline inside an XML document, or as an external reference.

Internal DTD Declaration

If the DTD is declared inside the XML file, it should be wrapped in a DOCTYPE definition with the following syntax:
<!DOCTYPE root-element [element-declarations]>
Example XML document with an internal DTD:

```
<?xml version="1.0"?>
<!DOCTYPE note [
<!ELEMENT note (to,from,heading,body)>
<!ELEMENT to (#PCDATA)>
<!ELEMENT from (#PCDATA)>
```

Advanced Web Tehnologies

```
<!ELEMENT heading (#PCDATA)>
<!ELEMENT body (#PCDATA)>
]>
<note>
<to>Tove</to>
<from>Jani</from>
<heading>Reminder</heading>
<body>Don't forget me this weekend</body>
</note>
```

The DTD above is interpreted like this:

!DOCTYPE note defines that the root element of this document is note
!ELEMENT note defines that the note element contains four elements:
"to,from,heading,body"
!ELEMENT to defines the to element to be of type
"#PCDATA"
!ELEMENT from defines the from element to be of type "#PCDATA"
!ELEMENT heading defines the heading element to be of type "#PCDATA"
!ELEMENT body defines the body element to be of type "#PCDATA"

External DTD Declaration

If the DTD is declared in an external file, it should be wrapped in a DOCTYPE definition with the following syntax:
```
<!DOCTYPE root-element SYSTEM "filename">
```

This is the same XML document as above, but with an external DTD:
```
xml version="1.0"?>
<!DOCTYPE note SYSTEM "note.dtd">
<note>
 <to>Tove</to>
 <from>Jani</from>
 <heading>Reminder</heading>
 <body>Don't forget me this weekend!</body>
</note>
```

And this is the file "note.dtd" which contains the DTD:
```
<!ELEMENT note (to,from,heading,body)>
<!ELEMENT to (#PCDATA)>
<!ELEMENT from (#PCDATA)>
<!ELEMENT heading (#PCDATA)>
<!ELEMENT body (#PCDATA)>
```

Why Use a DTD?

With a DTD, each of your XML files can carry a description of its own format.
With a DTD, independent groups of people can agree to use a standard DTD for interchanging data.
Your application can use a standard DTD to verify that the data you receive from the outside world is valid.
You can also use a DTD to verify your own data.

XML Schema

The purpose of an XML Schema is to define the legal building blocks of an XML document, just like a DTD.
An XML Schema:
    defines elements that can appear in a document
    defines attributes that can appear in a document
    defines which elements are child elements
    defines the order of child elements
    defines the number of child elements
    defines whether an element is empty or can include text
    defines data types for elements and attributes
    defines default and fixed values for elements and attributes

XML Schemas are the Successors of DTDs

We think that very soon XML Schemas will be used in most Web applications as a replacement for DTDs. Here are some reasons:
    XML Schemas are extensible to future additions
    XML Schemas are richer and more powerful than DTDs
    XML Schemas are written in XML
    XML Schemas support data types
    XML Schemas support namespaces

XML Schemas are much more powerful than DTDs.

XML Schemas Support Data Types

One of the greatest strength of XML Schemas is the support for data types.
With support for data types:
    It is easier to describe allowable document content
    It is easier to validate the correctness of data
    It is easier to work with data from a database
    It is easier to define data facets (restrictions on data)
    It is easier to define data patterns (data formats)
    It is easier to convert data between different data types

XML Schemas use XML Syntax

Another great strength about XML Schemas is that they are written in XML.
Some benefits of that XML Schemas are written in XML:
- You don't have to learn a new language
- You can use your XML editor to edit your Schema files
- You can use your XML parser to parse your Schema files
- You can manipulate your Schema with the XML DOM
- You can transform your Schema with XSLT

XML Schemas Secure Data Communication

When sending data from a sender to a receiver, it is essential that both parts
have the same "expectations" about the content.

With XML Schemas, the sender can describe the data in a way that the receiver
will understand.

A date like: "03-11-2004" will, in some countries, be interpreted as 3.November
and in other countries as 11.March.

However, an XML element with a data type like this:
<date type="date">2004-03-11</date>
ensures a mutual understanding of the content, because the XML data type
"date" requires the format "YYYY-MM-DD".

XML Schemas are Extensible

XML Schemas are extensible, because they are written in XML.
With an extensible Schema definition you can:
- Reuse your Schema in other Schemas
- Create your own data types derived from the standard types
- Reference multiple schemas in the same document

Well-Formed is not Enough

A well-formed XML document is a document that conforms to the XML syntax
rules, like:
- it must begin with the XML declaration
- it must have one unique root element
- start-tags must have matching end-tags
- elements are case sensitive
- all elements must be closed
- all elements must be properly nested
- all attribute values must be quoted
- entities must be used for special characters

Even if documents are well-formed they can still contain errors, and those errors can have serious consequences.

Think of the following situation: you order 5 gross of laser printers, instead of 5 laser printers. With XML Schemas, most of these errors can be caught by your validating software.

XPath

XPath is used to navigate through elements and attributes in an XML document. XPath is a major element in W3C's XSLT standard - and XQuery and XPointer are both built on XPath expressions.
XPath is a language for finding information in an XML document.

What is XPath?

XPath is a syntax for defining parts of an XML document
XPath uses path expressions to navigate in XML documents
XPath contains a library of standard functions
XPath is a major element in XSLT
XPath is a W3C recommendation

XPath Path Expressions

XPath uses path expressions to select nodes or node-sets in an XML document. These path expressions look very much like the expressions you see when you work with a traditional computer file system.

XPath Standard Functions

XPath includes over 100 built-in functions. There are functions for string values, numeric values, date and time comparison, node and QName manipulation, sequence manipulation, Boolean values, and more.

XPath is Used in XSLT

XPath is a major element in the XSLT standard. Without XPath knowledge you will not be able to create XSLT documents.
XQuery and XPointer are both built on XPath expressions. Xquery 1.0 and XPath 2.0 share the same data model and support the same functions and operators.

XPATH is a W3C Recommendation

XPath became a W3C Recommendation 16. November 1999.
XPath was designed to be used by XSLT, XPointer and other XML parsing software.

XSLT

XSLT(Extensible Stylesheet Language Transformation) is a language for transforming XML documents into XHTML documents or to other XML documents.
XPath is a language for navigating in XML documents.

What is XSLT?

XSLT stands for XSL Transformations
XSLT is the most important part of XSL
XSLT transforms an XML document into another XML document
XSLT uses XPath to navigate in XML documents
XSLT is a W3C Recommendation

XSLT = XSL Transformations

XSLT is the most important part of XSL.
XSLT is used to transform an XML document into another XML document, or another type of document that is recognized by a browser, like HTML and XHTML. Normally XSLT does this by transforming each XML element into an (X)HTML element.
With XSLT you can add/remove elements and attributes to or from the output file. You can also rearrange and sort elements, perform tests and make decisions about which elements to hide and display, and a lot more.
A common way to describe the transformation process is to say that XSLT transforms an XML source-tree into an XML result-tree.

XSLT Uses XPath

XSLT uses XPath to find information in an XML document.
XPath is used to navigate through elements and attributes in XML documents.

How Does it Work?

In the transformation process, XSLT uses XPath to define parts of the source document that should match one or more predefined templates. When a match is found, XSLT will transform the matching part of the source document into the result document.

XSLT is a W3C Recommendation

XSLT became a W3C Recommendation 16. November 1999.

SAX and DOM

SAX (Simple API for XML) is a serial access parser API for XML. SAX provides a mechanism for reading data from an XML document. It is a popular alternative to the Document Object Model (DOM).

XML processing with SAX

A parser which implements SAX (ie, *a SAX Parser*) functions as a stream parser, with an event-driven API. The user defines a number of callback methods that will be called when events occur during parsing. The SAX events include:
  XML Text nodes
  XML Element nodes
  XML Processing Instructions
  XML Comments

Events are fired when each of these XML features are encountered, and again when the end of them is encountered. XML attributes are provided as part of the data passed to element events.

SAX parsing is unidirectional; previously parsed data cannot be re-read without starting the parsing operation again.

Example
Given the following XML document:
```
<?xml version="1.0" encoding="UTF-8"?>
<RootElement param="value">
  <FirstElement>
    Some Text
  </FirstElement>
  <?some_pi some_attr="some_value"?>
  <SecondElement param2="something"> Pre-Text
    <Inline>Inlined text</Inline> Post-text.
  </SecondElement>
</RootElement>
```

This XML document, when passed through a SAX parser, will generate a sequence of events like the following:

  XML Element start, named *RootElement*, with an attribute *param* equal to "value"

  XML Element start, named *FirstElement*

  XML Text node, with data equal to "Some Text" (note: text processing, with regard to spaces, can be changed)

  XML Element end, named *FirstElement*

  Processing Instruction event, with the target *some_pi* and data *some_attr="some_value"*

XML Element start, named *SecondElement*, with an attribute *param2* equal to "something"

XML Text node, with data equal to "Pre-Text"

XML Element start, named *Inline*

XML Text node, with data equal to "Inlined text"

XML Element end, named *Inline*

XML Text node, with data equal to "Post-text."

XML Element end, named *SecondElement*

XML Element end, named *RootElement*

Note that the first line of the sample above is the XML Declaration and not a processing instruction; as such it will not be reported as a processing instruction event.

The result above may vary: the SAX specification deliberately states that a given section of text may be reported as multiple sequential text events. Thus in the example above, a SAX parser may generate a different series of events, part of which might include:

XML Element start, named *FirstElement*
XML Text node, with data equal to "Some "
XML Text node, with data equal to "Text"
XML Element end, named *FirstElement*

Benefits

SAX parsers have certain benefits over DOM-style parsers.
The quantity of <u>memory</u> that a SAX parser must use in order to function is typically much smaller than that of a DOM parser. DOM parsers must have the entire tree in memory before any processing can begin, so the amount of memory used by a DOM parser depends entirely on the size of the input data. The memory footprint of a SAX parser, by contrast, is based only on the maximum depth of the XML file (the maximum depth of the XML tree) and the maximum data stored in XML attributes on a single XML element.
Both of these are always smaller than the size of the parsed tree itself.

Because of the event-driven nature of SAX, processing documents can often be faster than DOM-style parsers. Memory allocation takes time, so the larger memory footprint of the DOM is also a performance issue.

Due to the nature of DOM, streamed reading from disk is impossible. Processing XML documents larger than main memory is also impossible with DOM parsers but can be done with SAX parsers. However, DOM parsers may make use of <u>disk space as memory</u> to sidestep this limitation.

Drawbacks

The event-driven model of SAX is useful for XML parsing, but it does have certain drawbacks.

Certain kinds of XML validation require access to the document in full. For example, a DTD IDREF attribute requires that there be an element in the document that uses the given string as a
DTD ID attribute. To validate this in a SAX parser, one would need to keep track of every previously encountered ID attribute and every previously encountered IDREF attribute, to see if any matches are made. Furthermore, if an IDREF does not match an ID, the user only discovers this after the document has been parsed; if this linkage was important to building functioning output, then time has been wasted in processing the entire document only to throw it away.

Additionally, some kinds of XML processing simply require having access to the entire document. XSLT and XPath, for example, need to be able to access any node at any time in the parsed XML tree. While a SAX parser could be used to construct such a tree, the DOM already does so by design.

DOM

What is the DOM?

The DOM is a W3C (World Wide Web Consortium) standard. The DOM defines a standard for accessing documents like XML and HTML. *"The W3C Document Object Model (DOM) is a platform and language-neutral interface that allows programs and scripts to dynamically access and update the content, structure, and style of a document."*

The DOM is separated into 3 different parts / levels:

- Core DOM - standard model for any structured document
- XML DOM - standard model for XML documents
- HTML DOM - standard model for HTML documents

The DOM defines the **objects and properties** of all document elements, and the **methods** (interface) to access them.

What is the HTML DOM?

The HTML DOM defines the **objects and properties** of all HTML elements, and the **methods** (interface) to access them.

If you want to study the HTML DOM, find the HTML DOM tutorial on our Home page.

What is the XML DOM?
The XML DOM is:
  A standard object model for XML
  A standard programming interface for XML
  Platform- and language-independent
  A W3C standard

The XML DOM defines the objects and properties of all XML elements, and the methods (interface) to access them.

In other words: The XML DOM is a standard for how to get, change, add, or delete XML elements.

QUESTIONS:

  What does XML stands for?
  What is the difference between XML and HTML?
  Which are the 5 predefined entity references in XML?
  What does DTD stands for?
  What is an XML schema? Explain.
  What is XPath? Explain.
  What does XSL stands for?
  What is XSLT? How does it work?
  What is SAX? Explain.
  What are different SAX events?
  What are the benefits of SAX over DOM?
  What are the drawbacks of SAX?
  What are the three different parts/levels of DOM?

9

AJAX

AJAX stands for Asynchronous JavaScript and XML. AJAX is a new technique for creating better, faster, and more interactive web applications with the help of XML, HTML, CSS, and Java Script.

Ajax uses XHTML for content, CSS for presentation, along with Document Object Model and JavaScript for dynamic content display.

Conventional web applications transmit information to and from the sever using synchronous requests. It means you fill out a form, hit submit, and get directed to a new page with new information from the server.

With AJAX, when you hit submit, JavaScript will make a request to the server, interpret the results, and update the current screen. In the purest sense, the user would never know that anything was even transmitted to the server.

XML is commonly used as the format for receiving server data, although any format, including plain text, can be used.

AJAX is a web browser technology independent of web server software.

A user can continue to use the application while the client program requests information from the server in the background.

Intuitive and natural user interaction. Clicking is not required, mouse movement is a sufficient event trigger.

Data-driven as opposed to page-driven.

Rich Internet Application Technology

AJAX is the most viable Rich Internet Application (RIA) technology so far. It is getting tremendous industry momentum and several tool kit and frameworks are emerging. But at the same time, AJAX has browser incompatibility and it is supported by JavaScript, which is hard to maintain and debug.

AJAX is Based on Open Standards

AJAX is based on the following open standards –
Browser-based presentation using HTML and Cascading Style Sheets (CSS).
Data is stored in XML format and fetched from the server. Behind-the-scenes data fetches using XMLHttpRequest objects in the browser.

JavaScript to make everything happen.

AJAX Technologirs

AJAX cannot work independently. It is used in combination with other technologies to create interactive webpages.

JavaScript
JavaScript function is called when an event occurs in a page.
Glue for the whole AJAX operation.

DOM
API for accessing and manipulating structured documents.
Represents the structure of XML and HTML documents.

CSS
Allows for a clear separation of the presentation style from the content and may be changed programmatically by JavaScript

XMLHttpRequest
JavaScript object that performs asynchronous interaction with the server.

How AJAX Works

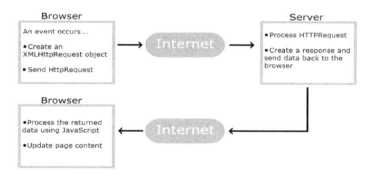

- 1. An event occurs in a web page (the page is loaded, a button is clicked)
- 2. An XMLHttpRequest object is created by JavaScript
- 3. The XMLHttpRequest object sends a request to a web server
- 4. The server processes the request
- 5. The server sends a response back to the web page
- 6. The response is read by JavaScript
- 7. Proper action (like page update) is performed by JavaScript

AJAX Example Explained Let AJAX change this text

HTML Page
```
<!DOCTYPE html>
<html>
<body>
<div id="demo">
 <h2>Let AJAX change this text</h2>
 <button type="button" onclick="loadDoc()">Change Content</button>
</div>
</body>
</html>
```

The HTML page contains a <div> section and a <button>.
The <div> section is used to display information from a server.
The <button> calls a function (if it is clicked).

Function loadDoc()

```
function loadDoc()
{
 var xhttp = new XMLHttpRequest();
 xhttp.onreadystatechange = function() {
  if (this.readyState == 4 && this.status == 200) {
   document.getElementById("demo").innerHTML = this.responseText;
  }
 };
 xhttp.open("GET", "ajax_info.txt", true);
 xhttp.send();
}
```

The function requests data from a web server and displays it:

AJAX Application
Here is a list of some famous web applications that make use of AJAX.

Google Maps
A user can drag an entire map by using the mouse, rather than clicking on a button.

* https://maps.google.com/

Google Suggest

As you type, Google offers suggestions. Use the arrow keys to navigate the results.

- https://www.google.com/webhp?complete=1&hl=en

Gmail

Gmail is a webmail built on the idea that emails can be more intuitive, efficient, and useful.

- https://gmail.com/

Yahoo Maps (new)

Now it's even easier and more fun to get where you're going!

- https://maps.yahoo.com/

Difference between AJAX and Conventional CGI Program

Try these two examples one by one and you will feel the difference. While trying AJAX example, there is no discontinuity and you get the response very quickly, but when you try the standard GCI example, you would have to wait for the response and your page also gets refreshed.

AJAX - Database Operations

To clearly illustrate how easy it is to access information from a database using AJAX, we are going to build MySQL queries on the fly and display the results on "ajax.html". But before we proceed, let us do the ground work. Create a table using the following command.

NOTE – We are assuming you have sufficient privilege to perform the following MySQL operations.

```
CREATE TABLE 'ajax_example' (
  'name' varchar(50) NOT NULL,
  'age' int(11) NOT NULL,
  'sex' varchar(1) NOT NULL,
  'wpm' int(11) NOT NULL,
  PRIMARY KEY ('name')
)
```

Now dump the following data into this table using the following SQL statements -

INSERT INTO 'ajax_example' VALUES ('Jerry', 120, 'm', 20);
INSERT INTO 'ajax_example' VALUES ('Regis', 75, 'm', 44);
INSERT INTO 'ajax_example' VALUES ('Frank', 45, 'm', 87);
INSERT INTO 'ajax_example' VALUES ('Jill', 22, 'f', 72);
INSERT INTO 'ajax_example' VALUES ('Tracy', 27, 'f', 0);
INSERT INTO 'ajax_example' VALUES ('Julie', 35, 'f', 90);

Client Side HTML File

Now let us have our client side HTML file, which is ajax.html, and it will have the following code -

```html
<html>
  <body>
    <script language = "javascript" type = "text/javascript">
      <!--
      //Browser Support Code
      function ajaxFunction() {
        var ajaxRequest;  // The variable that makes Ajax possible!

        try {
          // Opera 8.0+, Firefox, Safari
          ajaxRequest = new XMLHttpRequest();
        } catch (e) {

          // Internet Explorer Browsers
          try {
            ajaxRequest = new ActiveXObject("Msxml2.XMLHTTP");
          } catch (e) {

            try {
              ajaxRequest = new ActiveXObject("Microsoft.XMLHTTP");
            } catch (e) {
              // Something went wrong
              alert("Your browser broke!");
              return false;
```

```
      }
    }
  }

  // Create a function that will receive data
  // sent from the server and will update
  // div section in the same page.
  ajaxRequest.onreadystatechange = function() {

    if(ajaxRequest.readyState == 4) {
      var ajaxDisplay = document.getElementById('ajaxDiv');
      ajaxDisplay.innerHTML = ajaxRequest.responseText;
    }
  }

  // Now get the value from user and pass it to
  // server script.
  var age = document.getElementById('age').value;
  var wpm = document.getElementById('wpm').value;
  var sex = document.getElementById('sex').value;
  var queryString = "?age = " + age ;

  queryString +=  "&wpm = " + wpm + "&sex = " + sex;
  ajaxRequest.open("GET", "ajax-example.php" + queryString, true);
  ajaxRequest.send(null);
}
//-->

</script>
<form name = 'myForm'>
  Max Age: <input type = 'text' id = 'age' /> <br />
  Max WPM: <input type = 'text' id = 'wpm' /> <br />
  Sex:

  <select id = 'sex'>
    <option value = "m">m</option>
    <option value = "f">f</option>
  </select>

  <input type = 'button' onclick = 'ajaxFunction()' value = 'Query MySQL'/>
</form>
```

```
  <div id = 'ajaxDiv'>Your result will display here</div>
 </body>
</html>
```

NOTE – The way of passing variables in the Query is according to HTTP standard and have formA.

```
URL?variable1 = value1;&variable2 = value2;
```
The above code will give you a screen as given below –

Max Age: ☐

Max WPM: ☐

Sex: ☐ ▼

Your result will display here in this section after you have made your entry.

Server Side PHP File

Your client-side script is ready. Now, we have to write our server-side script, which will fetch age, wpm, and sex from the database and will send it back to the client. Put the following code into the file "ajax-example.php".

```php
<?php
$dbhost = "localhost";
$dbuser = "dbusername";
$dbpass = "dbpassword";
$dbname = "dbname";
//Connect to MySQL Server
mysql_connect($dbhost, $dbuser, $dbpass);
//Select Database
mysql_select_db($dbname) or die(mysql_error());
// Retrieve data from Query String
$age = $_GET['age'];
$sex = $_GET['sex'];
$wpm = $_GET['wpm'];
// Escape User Input to help prevent SQL Injection
$age = mysql_real_escape_string($age);
$sex = mysql_real_escape_string($sex);
$wpm = mysql_real_escape_string($wpm);
//build query
$query = "SELECT * FROM ajax_example WHERE sex = '$sex'";
if(is_numeric($age))
```

```
    $query .= " AND age <= $age";
if(is_numeric($wpm))
    $query .= " AND wpm <= $wpm";

//Execute query
$qry_result = mysql_query($query) or die(mysql_error());
//Build Result String
$display_string = "<table>";
$display_string .= "<tr>";
$display_string .= "<th>Name</th>";
$display_string .= "<th>Age</th>";
$display_string .= "<th>Sex</th>";
$display_string .= "<th>WPM</th>";
$display_string .= "</tr>";
// Insert a new row in the table for each person returned
while($row = mysql_fetch_array($qry_result)) {
    $display_string .= "<tr>";
    $display_string .= "<td>$row[name]</td>";
    $display_string .= "<td>$row[age]</td>";
    $display_string .= "<td>$row[sex]</td>";
    $display_string .= "<td>$row[wpm]</td>";
    $display_string .= "</tr>";
}
echo "Query: " . $query . "<br />";
$display_string .= "</table>";
echo $display_string;
?>
```

Now try by entering a valid value (e.g., 120) in *Max Age* or any other box and then click Query MySQL button.

Max Age:

Max WPM:

Sex: m

Your result will display here in this section after you have made your entry.

Thank You.....

Advanced Web Tehnologies